Anheuser-Busch, Inc.
ONE OF THE ANHEUSER-BUSCH COMPANIES

To My Fellow Irishmen,

It is with great enthusiasm and personal pride that I pass on the enclosed complimentary copy of "Dreamers of Dreams: Portraits Of the Irish in America."

Written by renowned Irish author Donal O'Donovan —whom I had the pleasure of meeting on his recent trip to St. Louis — the book is a "Who's Who" of notable Irish Americans, who are recognized for their personal accomplishments and appreciation of their Irish ancestry.

In that vein, I am most honoured to have been chosen among those who are featured in this book, including educators Brother John G. Driscoll, president of Iona College, and Sister Dorothy Ann Kelly, president of the College of New Rochelle; Irish American Cultural Institute President Eoin McKiernan; Joseph Roche, president of the Ancient Order of Hibernians; radio producer/broadcaster Dorothy Hayden; William J. Burke, senior vice president of the Bank of Ireland; and more than a dozen other truly special "green-blooded" Irishmen.

In closing, I sincerely hope you enjoy this book, which we hope you will find as fun and interesting reading.

Sincerely,

Dennis P. Long,
President, Anheuser-Busch, Inc.

ACKNOWLEDGMENTS

HELP, support and encouragement have been given to me in such abundance that it is remarkably hard to know where to begin to thank and impossible to devise a way of ending. To Seamas Daly who lived with the project from conception to parturition and wetnursed it beyond; to Jim Whitty who said "why not write a book about it?"; to Hilary Hough who showed more confidence than I had; to Sean McQuaid for endless encouragement and strength; to Jim McNamara who bought a pig in a poke; to Bill Maxwell who lent wings to the research; to Mick Dunne who gave so generously of time and material; to Mary Mullally who offered solace, wisdom and hard work; to Sheila Gallivan who took on the herculean task of typing the tome; to Lisa Hattin for warm responses to *cris de coeur*; to Peter Hooper, Jim O'Donnell and Pat Barry who supplied crutches when they were needed; to my daughters Kristin and Síofra and my wife and companion Jenny for loving support and hours of listening—to all these and more, I can say only heartfelt thanks.

Printed and bound in Ireland by Irish Printers Ltd.
Set in Times Roman by Computerset Ltd.
Designed by Kristin O'Donovan.
Picture research Seamas Daly.
Cover picture: drawn by Hughson Hawley, 1891.
Courtesy of the Library of Congress, Washington D.C.
Published in 1984.

Published by Kilbride Books, Kilbride Lodge, Bray, Co. Wicklow, Ireland.

ISBN 0 998018 003

DREAMERS OF DREAMS

PORTRAITS OF THE IRISH IN AMERICA

DONAL O'DONOVAN

PREFACE

"Pat arrived in America to find that not only were the streets not paved with gold; they were not paved at all—and *he* was expected to pave them". That was said in the 1830s, but in a sense it was true for at least another century to come. The Irish in America, after 150 years in which they were valued for their labour only, have only in the second half of the 20th century become totally accepted as wielders of real power.

It is widely though not universally acknowledged that John Fitzgerald Kennedy's achievement in becoming President of the United States broke the residual barrier, the lingering prejudice, that had prevented the ultimate assimilation of the Catholic Irishman into American society.

Evidence that the logjam is truly broken is provided by the fact that now, in the 1980s, at least 35 per cent of Corporate America is controlled by Irish Americans. Upward social mobility for so many was the result of initiative and education, and it is to the eternal credit of those who dreamed the American dream that their prosperity and power were created without the loss of their cultural identity as Irishmen.

This exercise of corporate power by the Irish of America is new. We have seen the Irish contribution to the labour unions; to the law enforcement agencies; to literature and acting; to the armed forces; to the business community, and of course to education and the Church. But as this series of portraits purports to show, a novel history is now being made. A different twist has been given to the aphorism that America was built by horse power, steam power and Irish power. It will be for the sociologist of the future to relate how "the movers and shakers" of this new world used their consciousness of the rich ethnic heritage, traditional values and transmitted attitudes of Ireland to form a satisfactory new world view.

These pages, by setting down in print the realisation of 25 Irish American dreams, reveal much about the dreamers.

DONAL O'DONOVAN
Kilbride Lodge
Bray
October, 1984

CONTENTS

FOREWORD

ALTHOUGH the stories told here are those of living Irish-American men and women, they are in the main stories rooted in the triumph over despair that was Ireland in America a century and more ago.

For the latter-day people of Ireland who may read what is set down in this unique book—unique because it has not been attempted before—the twenty five portraits in Donal O'Donovan's gallery will offer an insight into the ingredients of personal success and fulfilment, an insight into the nature of personal trust, family ties, the quest for learning and the careful tending of roots.

For the people of the Irish diaspora who may read about these dreamers and their dreams, the reality of being Irish will be renewed. At one level, this book is a journalist's work, an observer's *oeuvre*, well crafted and pretending to be no more than it is—a series of tales of different kinds of success in a different kind of world. At another level, perhaps, it will serve a higher purpose: to raise the profile and enhance the pride of this ancient race in its achievements abroad.

The Irish American, whom we call the *Poncánach* in Gaelic, has earned a special place in our hearts that he will yield to no man under God. He first won it during the American Revolution, became indispensable to the folk at home in the wake of the Famine and rallied to every national call since the Fenians. His nostalgic memories and proverbial generosity made him an easy target for all-comers—political leaders building up the national movement at home like Parnell, Davitt and Redmond, scores of bishops and priests seeking financial aid to complete their new churches from Armagh Cathedral in the middle of the last century to Galway in the middle of this one, Douglas Hyde appealing for the Gaelic League, Pádraig Pearse for St Enda's and de Valera for the *Irish Press*.

It used to be said that the aims of these movements were achieved through the pennies of the poor. The present book shows that those days are long past. In real estate and banking, in politics and the unions, in industry and the professions. These Irish emigrants and Irish Americans have gone right to the top. For the most part they are self-made. In standards of living, education and wealth the Irish in U.S.A. have already moved past most other European groups—perhaps only the Jews are still clearly ahead of them.

In the midst of many problems at home Ireland took much comfort recently from the discovery that 43 million Americans now claim some Irish blood, more than twice as many as was usually mentioned in the past. This was surpassed only by the Germans and the English. But German-Americans are still far less than the population of Germany and the English in U.S.A. are no more numerous than the English at home. But Irish-Americans outnumber the Irish at home by more than ten to one.

If this mighty power could be properly harnessed in support of the homeland—disciplined, united, irresistible—all our economic and political problems would be quickly solved. Donal O'Donovan's litany shows us where to begin, for these men are not only extremely influential across the Atlantic but have never forgotten their roots here. Perhaps there are, in truth, the *Séarlas Óg* and *Mac an Cheannaí* and *Buachaill Bán*, the Saviours of whom the poets sang and for whom earlier generations waited in vain.

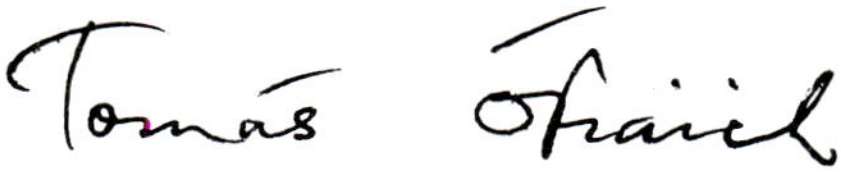

Tomás Ó Fiaich
Cardinal Archbishop of Armagh

INTRODUCTION

THERE is an epic quality to the story of the American Irish. Despite the difficulties and the dangers, the frustrations and the failures, the history of Irish-America over the past two centuries is essentially a success story. For much of the period, the fortunes of the American Irish stood in striking contrast to the fortunes of Ireland itself. Nevertheless, the histories of the Irish at home and the Irish in America are intimately intertwined. This is not, contrary to the impression conveyed by eager publicists, because the bulk of the American Irish devoted their lives to brooding on Ireland's fate. The vast majority of them were far too busy becoming good Americans to spend their time on evocative might-have-beens. Rather is it because the continuity of emigration from Ireland to America, and the transmission over so long a period of attitudes acquired in the ancestral culture, influenced significantly the response of immigrants to their American destiny. Inherited values cannot be sloughed off. They have to be adapted.

About seven million emigrants have left Ireland for America since 1700. More than five million of the 35 million Europeans who constituted the great wave of emigration to America in the century after 1820 came from Ireland. The most recent American census reports that no fewer than 42 million Americans acknowledge some Irish ancestry, a far higher figure than even propagandists imagined. Much of the Irish-American experience was common to all immigrants. But there were important distinctive features. Irish immigration lasted longest of any major immigrant flow. The heavy German emigration in the mid-19th century ground to a virtual halt by 1890. Swedish, Norwegian, Italian, Polish and Jewish emigration concentrated heavily on the immediate pre-1914 decades. Only the Irish seemed to keep going, generation after generation, over so long a period. For well over a century there was always a numerous first generation of Irish immigrants in America. The complexity of inter-generational relationships in the immigrant community remains to be fully explored. But it may be hazarded that it helps account for the remarkable cohesiveness of Irish America, which enabled it to punch its weight in American public life to a greater extent than numbers alone would have allowed.

First generation immigrants were particuarly solicitous about sending remittances back home. As late as 1910 these enabled 40 per cent of Irish emigrants to have their fares paid for them. The presence of first-generation immigrants also permitted Irish politicians to earn rich dividends from American fund raising activities, immigrant money often serving to lubricate the wheels of Irish political activity. The continuing immigration also permitted considerable inter-marriage between the generations in Irish-America, serving as a bridge across the years as well as across the ocean, linking time and place in a continuous flow of emotional experience. Irish attitudes could continue to be transmitted within the Irish-American community as the earlier generations were leavened by new arrivals, while these in turn were enabled to adapt in a relatively painless way through their assimilation into Irish-America. Immigrants became good Americans by first becoming good Irish-Americans.

Another powerful factor reinforcing the cohesiveness of the immigrant community was the unusual sex structure of Irish emigration. Males and females emigrated in equal proportions. This may seem normal. It wasn't. Men dominated European emigration to America, with a 2:1 majority over women. The virtually 50/50 ratio in Irish emigration permitted the Irish to inter-marry to a greater degree than was possible for many other immigrant peoples. It did more than that. The role of women in the history of Irish-America (as indeed in the history of Ireland) has been largely overlooked. It was probably central to many of the more distinctive features of the American Irish experience. It may, for instance, have significantly influenced settlement patterns. Despite their rural backgrounds, the Irish notoriously clung to the big cities. Many were doubtless compelled by poverty to remain in their place of arrival. Nevertheless, a great deal of internal migration did occur among the Irish in America. But they migrated more from town to town than from town to country. Even when they pushed inland, whether as canal or railroad builders, or towards Chicago or San Francisco, they still mainly opted for urban residence. Poverty alone cannot explain their overall settlement pattern. Most Irish girls emigrated as individuals, not in family groups. They accordingly enjoyed some discretion over their own lives on arrival in America, instead of having to tag along with male-dominated families. It seems likely that the girls, having acquired a modest income of their own from city employment, even if it was initially as despised domestics, simply refused to countenance the rigours of farming, knowing the backbreaking work that would be involved, and shrewdly anticipating whose backs were likely to be broken. The Catholic Church quickly came to play a cultural as well as a religious role for the vast majority of the American Irish. The church building itself became the physical hub of their universe, as well as a symbol of their identity and their resilience. The Irish soon came to dominate the upper echelons of the Church. They brought many assets with them. They had numbers, especially as they remained, or became, practising Catholics. They had clergy, often recruited directly from Ireland, for if they took their religion from Rome, they preferred, like other immigrant groups, to take their clergy from home. They had the English language, an inestimable advantage in the world of public discourse. Their proprietorial attitude towards the Church naturally roused resentment among other Catholic ethnics, but it wasn't until the mid-20th century that Polish and Italian clergy effectively asserted their claims to senior posts.

That the Irish occasionally behaved arrogantly during their period of dominance should not detract from their extraordinary achievement, in purely secular terms, in laying the foundations of the Catholic Church in 19th century America. The Church conducted the most extensive building programme of any single institution in the country. It established a school system, developed a health and welfare system, organised parishes, mobilised congregations. That remains the greatest and most enduring imperial achievement of the 19th century. Those who were tempted to accept the convenient assumption that the Irish lacked the administrative ability for self-government need have looked no further.

In politics, no less than in administration, the Irish made their mark. Daniel O'Connell, who ranks among the supreme political entrepreneurs of the modern world, had brought the Irish into the age of mass politics far in advance of the Europe of the time. Famine emigrants may have fled from a poverty stricken society, but by contemporary standards they were politically literate. O'Connell's political system proved remarkably suited to American conditions. A delicate perception of the possibilities of mass democratic politics distinguished the Irish electoral performance. And there were many election days, particularly in municipal politics, where the Irish quickly established an impressive ascendancy. If they took to American politics like ducks to water, they had their critics, for the water was murky enough in places. The main charge was that they exploited their electoral success more for factional gain than for public good. Even as sympathetic a scholar as

Senator Daniel Patrick Moynihan has suggested that 'The very parochialism and bureaucracy that enabled them to succeed in politics prevented them from doing much with government'. It is indeed ironic that in their dominance of New York city politics between the 1860s and the 1930s, the Irish, while throwing up a stream of bosses from Big Bill Tweed to Charles Murphy, failed to produce a mayor of the stature of the first Italian mayor, La Guardia. It remains conjectural to what extent this was a matter of genetic accident, or a function of the Irish political ethos. The hunger for style in a generation of better educated Irish-Americans, more sensitive to the charge of coarseness than their forebears, helps explain the emotive response of Irish-America to the rise of John Kennedy. For it was part of Kennedy's genius to simultaneously incorporate and yet transcend the traditional Irish political ethos. Irish-America had long enjoyed political power. It now sought status. It craved class. And Kennedy indubitably had class.

While a Kennedy would have been exceptional in any circumstances, significant changes were inevitable in Irish-American political culture. The key part played by the Irish as political brokers between immigrant America and the English speaking America had served its purpose. The capacity for coalition remained important in the welding together of a multi-ethnic American society. But as other immigrant groups became acculturated to the American way of life, they no longer needed the Irish to perform that role for them. A La Guardia in New York, or a Cermak in Chicago, had nothing to learn from the old masters. Their very success in integrating other immigrants into the American political process left the Irish in search of a new role.

Their rapidly rising educational levels since the Second World War had helped their adaptation to changing circumstances. The research of Andrew Greeley has shown that the Irish, traditionally anxious to put their children to work at an early age, thus depriving them of the chance of a college education, have now become one of the most education conscious groups in America. Their exceptional educational achievement, and their consequent conquest of responsible managerial and professional posts, have been the most distinctive features of their post-Second World War performance. The Irish achieved early dominance of the trade union movement, drawing on the organisational, political and brokerage skills that served them so well in religion and in politics. The significance of the recent achievement is that they have now broadened their occupational and power base to an extraordinary degree by their success across the whole spectrum of economic activity.

The portraits drawn by Donal O'Donovan vividly illustrate recent developments. The Irish in America to-day, even the first generation Irish, do not confront obstacles of prejudice and of poverty as intense as those overcome by earlier generations. Individuals, of course, may still have to surmount formidable challenges. It is indeed exhilarating to read of so many records of achievement in so many different fields of endeavour. To an educationalist it is encouraging to note the formative role of education in many of the careers chronicled here, and to observe the contribution of leading businessmen as benefactors of education. A professional educationalist in Ireland will gladly salute Brother Driscoll's achievement in transmuting Iona College. But he will also, recollecting the paralysing grip of existing Irish structures, grimace in envy at the opportunities afforded a dynamic educational entrepreneur in the American system.

Indeed, Donal O'Donovan's portraits must leave a bitter-sweet taste in the mouths, not only of Irish educationalists, but of Irish readers in general. The days when some Irish emigrants may have left for America to avoid tyranny are long past, at least in the Republic. The problem is no longer one of political oppression, but the more insidious ethic of complacency. One recurring theme throughout these chapters is the sense of frustration at the lack of opportunity in Ireland. The frustration, eloquently expressed by Kevin Roche, Bill Burke and Denis Kelleher, refers to the dreary decades of the forties and fifties, and it is true that giant strides have been taken since then to inject some vitality into Irish society.

But there is still a long distance to go to emulate the American ethic. Enriching in every sense though the American experience has been for these emigrants, the Irish at home can only wonder what type of country we might now have if their talents—and doubtless many more—had found an opportunity to fulfil their potential here. "America", says Bill Burke, "has been good to me. Where elso would a young fellow from Tubbercurry in Co, Sligo get to be a Vice President of a bank?" Until the answer to that question can be "Here, at home", Ireland will have failed to reap the full benefit of the Irish-American experience.

Joseph Lee

Joseph Lee is Vice-President of University College Cork and Professor of Modern History.

Michael Brosnan

MERRILL Lynch has been called "the first brokerage company in the nation to become a household name". It is the firm that brought Wall Street to Main Street and earlier in its history, when it had 31 general partners, was nicknamed "We the People" and "The Thundering Herd". It is the company that, on June 16th, 1957, gave the newly emigrated Michael Brosnan his first job.

Michael B. Brosnan, now a Vice President of Merrill Lynch, was born in 1933 in the small village of Gneeveguilla, near Rathmore, County Kerry, and not too far from Killarney. He was the third youngest of eleven children, seven of whom were girls. His father, who had fought with the Irish Guards regiment in France during World War I, worked in a creamery operated by the State-owned Dairy Disposals Board at Gullane.

Young Mike Brosnan was educated first at Gneeveguilla National School. This was no ordinary school, for in 1766, long before the National School system was conceived by an enlightened British Government, a school was opened in Gneeveguilla by one of Ireland's leading poets, Eoghan Ruadh Ó Súilleabháin (Owen Roe O'Sullivan). He was 18 when he opened his school but, as T.J. Barrington tells us in his "Discovering Kerry", within three years he had to flee the wrath of the parish priest. "One of Owen's most perfect lyrics is a lullaby he wrote when a local girl came into his school and left with him their baby, whose crying had to be stilled". Barrington, incidentally, spells the village Gneevegullia and the Ordnance Survey map, Gneevgullia.

From Gneeveguilla, Brosnan went to St. Brendan's College, Killarney, and then to All Hallows College, the Dublin seminary, where for 2½ years he studied for the priesthood. When he discovered that he did not have a vocation to serve God in that way, he got a job with the burgeoning firm of Dermot Ryan Car Hire for three months. But what Professor J.J. Lee has called "the pall of gloom that enveloped the 1950s" hung over Ireland, and Brosnan and thousands like him headed for Birmingham, England, where he worked for Dunlop the tyre makers at their Erdington plant. (Ironically, the Dunlop Rubber Company had its origin in the patent bought out in 1889 for the pneumatic tyre whose inventor, John Boyd Dunlop, was a veterinary surgeon practising in Belfast. The company had a factory in Cork until 1984).

Mike Brosnan was told he was "doing a good job" at Dunlops but he could not tolerate conditions in England, especially as he did not take alcohol, so in June, 1957, he joined the five members of his family already established in the United States. Two of his brothers had been through the Korean War, one of them, Seán, a transit worker, having been badly wounded and awarded the Purple Heart. The other brother, Frank, was in the Fire Department and died in 1983. He also had three sisters in the U.S. at the time and within two weeks he had obtained a job at Merrill Lynch, starting in the operations department where the volume was small but there was as yet no automation.

"They trained me all the way through", he says. "There was never any obstacle to my advancement". Charles Merrill and Winthrop Hiram Smith, appalled by the discovery during the war that the average age of their account executives was 52-plus, had decided to train their own. The first Training School class was held in 1945 and by the end of 1980 the firm had graduated 20,300 account executives.

When Mike Brosnan began, a team of five was keeping the stock record of Merrill Lynch, Pierce, Fenner and Smith, as the firm became known in 1958. (The story goes that when Charles Merrill was joined by Edmund Calvert Lynch in 1915, the printer forgot the comma in Merrill Lynch and Co. on their first stationery order and the partners could not afford to re-order). That team of five soon became a team of 180 and Brosnan became operations manager, overseeing a round-the-clock system.

At the same time the New York Stock Exchange had voted to permit member firms to incorporate and in January, 1959, "Inc". was added to the company's name, allowing more employee participation in its ownership. "The Thundering Herd" had 31 partners in 1940 and 71 in 1958. But by 1970 it had 1,400 stockholders and the next logical step—going public—came a year later when the rules were changed again.

About the same time, Merrill Lynch was given a role in buttressing the Wall Street structure. At the urgent request of the New York Stock Exchange, the company agreed late in 1970 to take over Goodbody and Company, one of the ten largest firms on Wall Street, because it was in serious trouble. It was laborious and risky but it worked, and that rescue and other activities provided a breathing spell for Wall Street.

The aura of danger brings one back in time to the Wall Street Crash of October, 1929, when the role of Merrill Lynch was quite extraordinarily prescient. President Reagan's Secretary of the Treasury, Donald T. Regan, who was Chairman and Chief Executive of Merrill Lynch and Co., Inc., the holding company, when he delivered a notable address on the company's history to the distinguished Newcomen Society on December 4th, 1980 (one week before he was designated a member of the President's Cabinet) has told the story of Charles Merrill's thoughts and actions with remarkable skill:

"His firm and investments were doing well, but by the late 20s Merrill was getting worried by the speculative excesses of the stock market boom. In 1928 he wrote his customers: 'Now is the time to get out of debt . . . . . Sell enough securities to lighten your obligations or pay them off entirely'.

"He found so little credence among knowledgeable financial people, he was beset by serious self-doubts and consulted a psychiatrist. After unburdening himself during several sessions, Charlie, on his next visit, found the doctor eagerly shoving at him a set of brokerage statements. The physician had followed the patient's prescription and sold his stockholdings. His diagnosis of Charlie: 'If you're crazy, then so am I'.

"Evidently, Merrill had more trouble convincing his own partners. In February, 1929, he wrote a stern letter to Lynch, which I have personally read, insisting he would brook no further delay in sharply reducing the firm's exposure: 'The financial skies are not clear...I do not like the outlook and I do not like the amount of money we owe'. Lynch received the letter en route to Europe. He replied from Paris along the line of: 'I don't agree with your thinking, but I will not disagree with your actions. If you wish, please sell all of my holdings'.

"Merrill Lynch and a good many of its customers had trimmed their sails sufficiently to absorb the 1929 buffeting . . . . " said Regan, whose address to the Newcomen Society was later printed by Princeton University Press.

The society's name perpetuates the work of Thomas Newcomen (1663–1729), the British pioneer whose valuable contributions to improving the newly invented steam engine brought him lasting fame in the field of mechanic arts. The Newcomen engines, used from 1712 to 1775, paved the way for the Industrial Revolution and Newcomen's inventive genius preceded by more than 50 years the brilliant work in steam done by James Watt.

A branch of the Newcomen family owned Newcomen's Bank in Dublin and was led, in the person of Sir William Gleadowe Newcomen, Bt., to vote for the Union of Ireland and England in 1800. The price of his vote, said Sir Jonah Barrington at the time, was "a peerage, the patronage of his county, and the pecuniary pickings also received by himself". He was the butt of a bitter broadsheet:

Though many years I've lived in Town
As New-come-In I'm only known.

A Dublin office of Merrill Lynch, Pierce, Fenner and Smith was mooted in the 1960s but for some reason the idea was not pursued, though the firm has over 60 offices in 26 foreign countries. From a total of 42 offices in 1940, Merrill Lynch now has over 400 securities offices in the United States alone, and abroad the company also has an active presence in investment and merchant banking and dealing in money market instruments. With strategic locations in financial centres throughout the time zones, Merrill Lynch offers round-the-clock as well as round-the-globe services.

As Mike Brosnan puts it: "It's a financial supermarket. Our most recent service, the Cash Management Account (CMA), propelled us to the top, outstripping the competition and yielding us over one million accounts.

"By combining a margin account, a money fund, and a Visa Card with cheque-writing privileges, CMA allows investors to keep their money (and credit) at work at all times, and yet instantly accessible. A prominent financial writer has called CMA 'maybe the most important financial innovation in years'".

Brosnan became a Vice President in 1980, and is registered to sell all over the country. He calls his colleagues "fine human beings, beautiful guys", referring to Roger Birk, who retired as Chairman and as Chief Executive Officer in July, 1984, and William Schreyer, who succeeded Birk. Schreyer, who was President until he became Chief Executive Officer, has announced "a major restructuring of the whole corporation" which presumably means a cost-cutting exercise. Costs were up by 17 per cent in the year to the end of March, 1984, and since then have seemed to be under better control. Merrill Lynch, the world's biggest stockbrokers, grew fast in the three years after Donald Regan became Secretary to the Treasury and had to relinquish his position. Under Birk, revenues rose from $3 billion in 1980 to $5.7 billion in 1983, while shareholders' equity doubled.

Mike Brosnan met Anne McGarrity of Cookstown, County Tyrone, when he was in England, and they were married in America in July, 1958. They have four children. Bernadette, who is 24, is a teacher and married to Tom Twomey in the Fire Department. Noreen's husband Danny Mulvanerty, is in the Police Department in Rockaway, New York. Edmund (20) is studying law and majoring in English at Fordham University in the Bronx, New York; and Brenda Anne (16) is a junior in the Dominican Academy in New York City.

Brosnan is a member of the Ancient Order of Hibernians, the Irish American Unity Conference (whose economic seminar on Ireland he attended in San Antonio, Texas, in May, 1984); the Kerrymen's Association of New York, the Knights of Columbus, the Chairmen's Club in Merrill Lynch, and the Flax Trust which aims to bring industry to the Ardoyne district of Belfast.

On one of his visits to Ireland he was interviewed by the nationally known radio personality, Donncha Ó Dúlaing. He goes usually to Kerry, where his brother Pat is retired from the Fry Cadbury chocolate crumb factory in Rathmore, and to Dublin, where he has as many relatives as he has in Kerry. He also visits his sister Joan who is in charge of the Presentation Convent in Drogheda and at present is doing her master's degree in Gonzaga College, Spokane, in Washington State, where Bing Crosby studied.

Because Mike Brosnan is married to a Northern Ireland girl, he has a special interest in the welfare of the North. He saw the Ardoyne devastation on a visit in 1978, and looked at the utter hopelessness on the people's faces. One result of his visit was that he helped to raise money to ban the use of plastic bullets by the Royal Ulster Constabulary and the British Army.

William Rogers, Senior Partner in Rogers and Wells; a member of the Board of Directors of Merrill Lynch and Co., and a former Secretary of State and Attorney General of the United States, introduced Donald T. Regan to the members of the Newcomen Society with a little story that could have applied to Mike Brosnan. He said: "When Don was still an up and coming Merrill Lynch Vice President, he made the front page of the *New York Times* testifying about a once-hot little company which some West Coast account executives had pushed without proper research. When the S.E.C. lawyer asked Don: 'What happened?' Don said: 'We goofed'.

"Candour, courage and integrity are his hallmarks".

WILLIAM J. BURKE

"I had never used a phone before. You have to remember that. Yet I was expected to produce day one". The speaker is William J. Burke, now Senior Vice President of the Bank of Ireland in New York, and he is talking of his first day in his first job in America.

The story begins in Tubbercurry, County Sligo, where Bill Burke was born into a family of eleven children. That was in 1941. His father, a "returned Yank", built the first garage business in the town in the 1920s and now the family has two garages.

Burke went to school in St. Nathy's College, Ballaghaderreen (where the discipline, he claims, is the best training for Wall Street). In the Ireland of the 1960s he could see no place for himself and when his father asked him: "Would you like to work in the garage?", he said he was sick of mending punctures and had no desire to spend the rest of his life in the family business.

So he wrote to one of his sisters in America and she "took out the papers" for him. His first visit to Dublin was for the medical examination in the consulate, and two weeks later he was on an Aer Lingus plane for New York. The passengers had to overnight in Gander, Newfoundland, because of bad weather and it was midweek when he reached New York.

There his brother-in-law got him a job in the Marine Midland Bank and by Monday he was at work. There were no Irish-born people in the bank so the management put him in the international department, dealing with letters of credit. The supervisors were mainland Chinese and other foreigners. One used an abacus and none spoke good English. They were not tolerant of the strange young Irishman who had been foisted on them.

"I never really conquered that job", he recalls. "The pressure was high; the phones rang all the time. I was living on 90th Street at Third Avenue with a few laid back Irish bus-drivers and the contrast got to me, especially the day there was a big snowfall and I was the only one who went to work. That was a baptism of fire.

"So I asked for a transfer to the credit department. I was a natural, took to it at once, and began to go to lectures at the American Institute of Banking at night. I did four years of night school and graduated from the American Institute of Credit as well.

"In the six years I was in the job I became pretty good at credit analysis, but I was not going any place. They thought I had a cute Irish brogue and they'd say things they'd learned from the movies like Erin go Breagh or top of the mornin' to you.

"Plus the money was not good, so I always had an outside job doing sales and credit approvals for furniture companies. I would either sell direct or extend credit on the merchandise and I became very good at that.

"Then my brothers asked me to open a garage in New York City with them. I was a silent partner in Burke's Foreign Car Service. They were experts on cars...

"In 1967 I began to take banking seriously and I joined the Franklin National Bank of New York, a country bank that came in from Long Island looking for talent. I went on an executive training programme and after two years became a corporate calling officer.

"I was low man on the totem pole so I got New York and New Jersey. I found that I was very good at talking to people and I was highly regarded by the federal regulators. I got involved in large loan approvals and became an assistant vice president.

"The bank grew to become one of the top 20 but by 1973 I became aware that the bank was not doing too well, borrowing heavily to keep liquid. I hung in there and the Federal Deposit Insurance Corporation got a buyer for the bank.

"I went away on vacation and returned three weeks later to find that massive staff cutbacks had been ordered. I had a choice: leave, or manage a country branch in Suffolk County 100 miles away.

"I knew the vice chairman of Barclays Bank vaguely, so I rang him with the story. 'How would you like to come work for us?' he asked me, and in 17 minutes I had a job. I was only 32 and I was able to leave a space for an older man who would not be so mobile.

"Barclays had just taken over a small country bank in Westchester County and I became Barclay's Regional Vice President there. I established a fine relationship with the people of the community and especially the Irish. I was well received by both bank and customers and I got salary increases and promotion. I remember someone asking me how does a British bank like Barclays treat you? and I answered: 'Warmly'.

"The Bank of Ireland had opened a representative office for its corporate clients in New York in 1971 and I knew Pat O'Hara there. I had a real desire to get into an Irish bank and I knew no bank was serving the Irish community, whereas other countries' banks were taking care of corporate business but also looking after their own.

"In the middle of 1977 I met Jack Stanley who headed up the International Department of the Bank of Ireland. Even though no money was discussed, I accepted his offer. By the time we opened our doors to the public early in 1978 I had developed my strong relationship with the Irish community. I knew the county associations, Gaelic Park—I was president of the Minor Board of the Gaelic Athletic Association six months previously—and the Ancient Order of Hibernians.

"It is normal in America to give free gifts such as clock radios to new depositors, but we went down the road of real quality Irish products—Belleek china, Royal Tara porcelain, Waterford, Cavan and Galway crystal. In one month we had a bank of a nice size", Bill Burke says proudly.

An American business magazine of the time said of the premises: "In a business where location is extremely important, the Bank of Ireland would be hard pressed to do better than its ground-floor showcase on Fifth Avenue. A cherished symbol of the Irish in America—St. Patrick's Cathedral—is diagonally across the street. Also nearby is a shopping district which cannot help but support a retail banking operation. Standing at the bank's front door, one's line of vision takes in the cathedral steps—and the display windows of Saks Fifth Avenue".

Burke points out that "a lot of our clients are not Irish but Jewish, Italian, German. We might be thought to be an ethnic bank but actually it's very mixed". Nonetheless, he assiduously cultivates the Irish connection and is a prominent member of the Ancient Order of Hibernians, the United Irish Foundation (a charitable organisation); the American Irish of Westchester County, and the Friendly Sons of St. Patrick, as well as his beloved Gaelic Athletic Association.

He receives five or six plaques a year from various Irish organisations and in 1984 he was the recipient of the Campbell-Houlihan Award given by the Donegal Football Club in recognition of his work for Gaelic games in New York. "Music", said the announcement of the club's banquet, "will be provided by the Shamrock Express".

Bill Burke says that his bank chose, because of the large

Irish-American community, to sponsor a rather esoteric sport—Gaelic football, which is played by over 2,000 American boys under 18 years of age in the greater New York area. These minors produce a team which is taken to Ireland to participate in the All-Ireland championships. In addition the parent bank in Ireland sponsors the American tour of the Bank of Ireland All Stars who are chosen by the cream of the Irish sporting press from the top Gaelic football and hurling players in Ireland.

"I don't think there's a pub in New York that doesn't bank with me", says Burke. "We also give things back, not only to the Gaelic Athletic Association but in the form of trophies for other competitions and prizes for *feiseanna* or other musical events. We probably patronise 90% of all the Irish dances that are held and most of all, we help the Irish community in times of death or other tragedy by supporting the family.

"They say I get 100 telephone calls a day and meet someone every 15 minutes. Some 80% of our work is not direct deposit taking: it's giving financial advice. We have a reputation in that area".

Bill Burke is married to the former Kathleen Beglan of Edgeworthstown, County Longford, who used to work for Chase Bank. They have four children, of whom Bill junior is the eldest. Bill is taking business and computer studies at Iona College, New Rochelle, where the Burkes live. Elizabeth (aged 17) and Michele (aged 15) are at the Ursuline Academy in the town, and Robert (10) is at the local grammar school.

The Burke children are Americans but they nurture a high regard for Irish culture and they love traditional Irish music and dances. They go to Ireland often for holidays and to see their grandmother, who now lives in Mullahoran, County Cavan. Burke's time with the children is valuable to him, but he finds he cannot help with their homework.

He has two brothers and a sister in New York. One brother is an engineer on the New York to Philadelphia train, the other runs a company on Wall Street, while his sister works in a savings bank.

"America", says Bill Burke, "has been good to me. Where else would a young fellow from Tubbercurry in County Sligo get to be vice president of a bank?"

Patrick J. Campbell

"I HAVE never known a genuine carpenter who was not prideful in his work; gentle, forthright and humane in his nature. Carpenters are mysteriously likely to be men of intelligence and integrity; they are at once visionary and realistic . . . . It just could be that the still living tonic of the long-felled trees clears the workman's brain and steadies his nerves and makes his hand sure and deft". This warm tribute came from the pen of Edna Ferber, the novelist, and while it may be over-romantic it does not conceal the fact that from the very beginning, carpenters were crucial to the growth and well-being of America.

Patrick J. Cambell, General President of the United Brotherhood of Carpenters and Joiners of America, is in his second year of office in a union that ten years ago had 850,000 members and is the largest construction union in the world. Campbell says: "I'm known as the Irishman throughout all the locals. I am the first Catholic Irishman to have reached this position".

His is an ancient and honourable craft, chronicled during the Pilgrim Fathers' first Christmas when all able-bodied men went ashore, "some to fell timber, some to saw, some to rive and some to carry, so no man rested all that day".

Carpenters were among the first craftsmen to organise associations which were the forerunners of today's trade unions. In 1724, the Carpenters' Company of Philadelphia was founded to establish "a book of prices". In 1773, members of the Ship Carpenters and Caulkers Club of Boston dressed as Indians, so tradition has it, and dumped tea into Boston Harbour—the famous "Boston Tea Party" that led to the American Revolution. It was in the Carpenters' Hall in Philadelphia that the Declaration of Independence was signed in 1776.

In Philadelphia also, in 1791, the house carpenters decided that: "In future, a Day's Work, amongst us, shall be deemed to commence at six o'clock in the morning, and terminate, at six in the evening of each day". The Master Carpenters refused and the journeymen laid down their tools in what may have been the first strike in America for shorter hours. Higher pay claims later led to the evolution of a legal doctrine holding that workers acting in concert to raise wages were engaged in a criminal conspiracy under Common Law. This doctrine, which as Charles O. Gregory has said "made labor unionists conform to the principles of classic economics", was not set aside until 1842.

Carpenters and other journeymen faced many uphill struggles, for the abolition of imprisonment for debt, for universal free education, currency and land reforms. In 1865, the ship caulkers of San Francisco won the first ever eight-hour day, but the end of the Civil War and the consequent flooding of the labour market saw a reversion to lower wages and worse conditions aggravated by the introduction of the first machines and the practice of piecework.

This dismal scene was transformed by Peter J. McGuire, the son of Irish immigrant parents who at 17 joined the Cabinet Makers' Union of New York. He was red-headed, ebullient, a rich baritone, fluent in German and a founder of the Social Democratic Party of North America. In March of 1881, he founded *The Carpenter* in St. Louis, Missouri, with his friend August Oberbeck editing the German edition. (The German language section persisted until America joined the war against Germany in 1917, and though the anti-German feeling of the time was the immediate cause, the decline in German-born membership of the United Brotherhood would soon have led to the same result).

A month later, in April, 1881, McGuire was elected secretary of a "Provisional Committee of the Carpenters' and Joiners' National Union" and in August a convention of 2,042 craftsmen from eleven cities decided in Chicago to form the United Brotherhood of Carpenters and Joiners of America, with Gabriel Edmonston of Washington, D.C., as General President, and McGuire as General Secretary. The Brotherhood was on its way.

"If the strong combine", wrote McGuire in the first issue of *The Carpenter*, "why should not the weak?", and after a false start he spread his championship of the worker to the formation in 1886 of the American Federation of Labor, with his close friend Samuel Gompers, a young cigar maker, as its first President. Gompers was to hold the post for 37 terms.

The Brotherhood's early victories, especially on shorter hours, met with hostility from both press and public and with stiff resistance from employers, especially when an economic downturn coincided. Then came the Panic of 1893, mass unemployment aided by a wave of immigration. It was 1907 before the eight-hour day was firmly established. Peter McGuire, the architect of the labour movement, was a year dead.

William Levi Hutcheson, "Big Bill", was the son of a Scotch-Irish ship caulker in Bay County, Michigan. He rose to the Presidency of the Brotherhood in 1915 and gave 36 years of distinguished service. The Great War offered a ready-made opportunity to organise the unorganised and extend the closed shop. The employers countered with the plea that Hutcheson had a patriotic duty to accept the open shop. It seemed to be patriotic for employers to make huge profits out of the war but unpatriotic of labour to seek justice. The solution was a National War Labor Board which involved solid gains for labour and a new personal friend for Hutcheson—former President William Howard Taft, whose grandson, William Howard Taft III, was United States Amabssador to Ireland in the early 1950s and was present at the switching on of electric power to the village of Bansha, County Tipperary.

When the war ended, the big industries were cash-rich and decided to get rid of collective bargaining, restrictions on hours of work and high wages. In a word, to smash the unions. To do so, they devised the American Plan based on the "right to work". Their doors, as they put it, were open to everyone seeking employment, and they coined the phrase "the open shop". It was a dirty campaign involving pressure on reluctant firms and manipulation of the public so that the union concept of the closed shop was deemed "un-American".

But the United Brotherhood, with 366,000 members and $700,000 in surplus cash, was ready with a new strategy. Hutcheson ordered cement from Belgium, timber from independent mills, trucks to operate quarries and gravel beds. These he offered to contractors willing to hire union labour, and soon the power of the bosses' organisation, the Industrial Association, began to crumble. But it was 1924 before the American Plan was finally broken, mainly by the Brotherhood.

After the stock market crash of 1929, wages were slashed and by 1933 nearly 13 million were out of work. Of United Brotherhood members, less than 30 per cent were employed, and large numbers could not pay their dues. But all was not black. The Wagner Act reaffirmed the worker's right to organise and declared it to be public policy to encourage collective bargaining. The Brotherhood in this grim depression paid out nearly $12 million in benefits.

Lumber workers on the West Coast were never effectively organised until the A.F.L. in 1934 gave the United Brotherhood of Carpenters and Joiners jurisdiction over them. The operators resisted unionisation and there was a bitter six-week confrontation in 1935, ending with a decent wage, safety standards and a vast improvement in conditions in the camps. The affiliated union is the Lumber Production Industrial Workers' Union.

World War II saw the Brotherhood still led by William Hutcheson who was determined to abide by the lessons learned in 1917-18. The Brotherhood played a remarkable role in helping the Allied victory, as is shown by its swift response to a critical shortage of trained carpenters which developed at two key war plants. A letter from the Under Secretary of War to President Hutcheson says in part:

"Your assistance in recruiting skilled mechanics to help build the Clinton and Hanford projects was an important factor in rushing these projects to completion and making it possible to drop the first atomic bomb on Japan . . . ." Membership soared from under 320,000 in 1940 to over 700,000 by war's end.

A spectacular victory was won by the Brotherhood in the fight waged against labour by the Department of Justices's anti-trust campaign. The issue was: Are the actions of labour organisations subject to the provision of the Anti-Trust Act? Finally in 1942, the Supreme Court said no.

But labour suffered an equally spectacular set back after the war when the Taft-Hartley Act established a manual of "don'ts" for unions, the most onerous provision being the one which in effect authorises states to pass compulsory open shop laws. Nineteen states took advantage of the invitation and organised labour has not yet had it overturned.

The building in which Patrick J. Campbell now presides over the destinies of the Brotherhood is just across the road from the Capitol in Washington, D.C. It was purpose-built in 1961 and was a recognition of the fact that the union's affairs could no longer be negotiated and conducted from Indianapolis. There is also a research office in Toronto, Canada. Delegates from Hamilton, Ontario, attended the founding meeting in Chicago in 1881 and Canadian membership has grown steadily ever since.

Maurice Hutcheson stepped into his father William's shoes in 1952 and retired 20 years later to hand over to William Sidell, who oversaw the affiliation in 1979 of the Wood, Wire and Metal Lathers International Union before retiring at the end of that year.

William Konyha served the traditional rigorous apprenticeship for the general presidency and it was he who spearheaded the celebration of the Brotherhood's centenary in 1981, when Pat Campbell was First

General Vice President. He recalls Konyha's words in the centenary year: "The job of the next one hundred years is the unfinished work of the first one hundred years". Thomas R. Brooks has documented the century of conflict in his exciting history of the Brotherhood, "The Road to Dignity".

Patrick J. Campbell's father was from Kiltormer, Ballinasloe, County Galway, and his mother from Eyrecourt in the same county. He has relations in Kiltormer, in Dublin, and in Kenmare, County Kerry, and they all received a visit in 1984 after Pat represented the A.F.L.—C.I.O at the British Trade Union Congress in Brighton, England, in September.

He was born in 1918 at 326 East 40th Street and went to school at St. Gabriel's (a tunnel goes through it now); Holy Name School, and Yorkville Elementary Junior High. He did one year of continuation school, which involved going to school one day a week from 8.30 to noon to learn typing. That ended with his 16th birthday. Orphaned at the age of six, he was the youngest of six boys and did his share of providing for the house by shining shoes, selling papers and working in a sweet factory.

At the age of 20, Pat moved to Rockland County, New York, and got a job at Rockland State Hospital. Then the war came and he served four years with the U.S. Army Air Force in the South Pacific.

Starting as an apprentice in Local Union 964, Rockland County, of the United Brotherhood of Carpenters and Joiners, he quickly became a journeyman carpenter, foreman, and superintendent before he was elected President of Local 964 in 1954. A year later, President Maurice Hutcheson appointed him to the international organising staff and in 1957 he was assigned to the Niagara Power Project, one of the largest contruction jobs in the world, where he gained a valuable insight into giant construction as chairman of the labour-management committee for the entire operation.

After 37 years of working upwards in his union, Pat Campbell reached the top in November, 1982, when William Konyha retired. He has served on several major boards and councils, has been a member of the Federal Committee on Apprenticeship and has received many awards and honours, including in 1984 the Medal of Honour of the Irish National Caucus.

He is married to the former Catherine Keane and they have three children. Patrick is an attorney in Rockland County, New York, and had Governor Mario Cuomo as one of his law professors at St. John's

University. Cynthia was a journalist with the New York *Daily News* and now is married to Terry McGuire and living in Virginia Beach, Virginia. Kevin is the legislative advocate of the United Brotherhood. ("Nepotism?" asks Pat Campbell. "I call it taking care of your own".) His eldest grandson goes to Villanova University in 1984. "Everything I missed in education I want to see they get. My wife—we've been married for 44 years—is a trooper. She's the boss, very pro-labour, like all my family. They all know the difference between right and wrong".

Pat Campbell and his son are active Walter Mondale supporters. "Ronald Reagan is a song and dance man, jumping from arms control to birth control. He has taken all the labour laws and by regulation he has changed them. He hasn't done a thing for working people. The Brotherhood had 850,000 members. Now we've lost 200,000 through Reagan.

"We have this serious long-running strike between our affiliate the L.P.I.W. and Louisiana-Pacific Corporation, which wants a union-free environment to make their plywood and waferboard products. It began in June, 1983 and there are 1,500 on strike throughout the U.S. with strike breakers at work and pickets being beaten. We have a nationwide consumer boycott of L.-P. products".

Louisiana-Pacific is the second-largest lumber producer in the United States, and the 18 plants affected are in California, Oregon, Washington, Idaho and Alaska. According to Evadna Linn, a timber analyst at Merrill Lynch, Pierce, Fenner and Smith, the personalities of Harry Merlo, Chairman and President of L.-P., and James Bledsoe, Executive Secretary of the Lumber Production Industrial Workers' Union, are a major factor in the strike. "Both are very strong men, very opinionated and unlikely to settle unless it's forced up from the ranks.... Merlo is probably the best operator in the business when it comes to understanding how to get the most out of a set of assets".

According to a local food bank worker, "people are coming in in tears. One woman said: 'My husband has always provided for us. This is the first time we have been without food'".

The original cause of the dispute, now almost lost in the cloud of violence and rhetoric, was the refusal of Louisiana-Pacific to honour an agreement struck between the union and the "Big Seven" sawmill companies giving a wage freeze for 1983, 4 per cent in 1984 and 4½ per cent in 1985. Harry Merlo contends that years of generous settlements have made Western timber less competitive than in the South, where wages are half as high. John Hubner in a report in the *San Jose Mercury*

News in February, 1984, said the union is not going to win because unions are seen as greedy and self-serving. "They defeated titans like Henry Ford and Andrew Carnegie. But if they don't come up with new tactics for the 80s—if they try to beat the Harry Merlos with weapons from the good old days—people like striker Dave Bigby will be fighting in vain". Harry Merlo does not give interviews.

Wearing his Irish American hat, Pat Campbell is a member of the Knights of Columbus, third degree; a member of the Ancient Order of Hibernians and the Friendly Sons of St. Patrick and a past president of the Holy Name Society. He believes that "Congressman Mario Biaggi is the best P.R. man the Irish have here. All the Four Horsemen—Moynihan, Carey, O'Neill and Kennedy—can say is: Stop sending money to the I.R.A. That money is not going for guns. Mike Flannery is a great man who has done a lot for Ireland. I was guest of honour at the Noraid dinner in 1980. I don't try to cause dissension. I do what I have to do and form my own opinions.

"Travel? I go all over. In February, 1983, I did 32,000 miles in a month. I made seven trips to the West Coast last year. I suppose I would do better than 100,000 miles a year. I spent a lot of time with the late Mickey Mullen of the Irish Transport and General Workers' Union. And George Lamon of the Irish Woodworkers and Machinists. They were both out here".

Patrick J. Campbell, whose term of office ends in 1986, is a short, stocky, pugnacious-looking Irishman whose final thought is for the West Coast strikers as he learns that an A.F.L.—C.I.O. food bank is on the way to Washington State and Oregon to help the hungry families. "Strike benefit is tough to keep up", he says. "We in the Brotherhood have put in about $2 million so far from Washington, D.C., and the area council for the western states has contributed about maybe $3.5 million".

Mike Carty

COUNTY Leitrim, where Michael Carty comes from, is the poorest county in Ireland, with a population exactly half that of neighbouring Counties Sligo, Roscommon, and Cavan. His people were small farmers at Aughavas, near Mohill, and in 1960, when Mike was 18, the whole family came to New York where his two older sisters had settled earlier. It is a classic story of emigration, topped off with the phenomenal success of Mike Carty in building up a chain of lucrative public houses and restaurants in Manhattan and reinvesting back in Ireland where he co-owns an award-winning pub in Limerick.

Mike went to the local National School and then to the Technical School in Mohill. At the height of Ireland's worst haemorrhage of emigration in modern times, he joined "McAlpine's Fusiliers", that vast army of Irishmen who found jobs in the construction industry in England, then dominated by Sir Robert McAlpine's firm. He spent 18 months in the building and public-house trades until the momentous decision was taken that his parents, his brother and himself should join his sisters in New York. The farm was let on the conacre system, the Irish system of 11-month tenure which ensures that the ownership remains in the family. Later, the holding was sold.

In New York, it was back to construction work again for five years as a labourer and a steel worker, living with his brother and another fellow in an apartment and going at night to Delahunts, "the equivalent of high school, at East 14th Street".

With his savings Mike opened a place in Monroe, New York, where he was "bouncer, bartender and porter, served a bit of food and brought in bands at the weekend. The place was beside the New Jersey border and the legal age limit in New Jersey was higher than in New York, so the young people came every weekend and there were constant fights. That was in 1966 until 1969. I had a couple of New York cops up every weekend doing nixers in Hennessy's Inn as we called it. Eventually I sold out".

Then Carty "hooked up" with Austin Delaney of Mayo and he is still with him. They opened the Blarney Star near the World Trade Center to serve the construction workers with food and drink, and in

1970 they opened a second Blarney Star. The next step was to buy a building in Murray Street and an adjoining building, open Rosie O'Grady's (Number one of the name) and sell the Blarney Star. In 1983-84 Mike spent $500,000 renovating that Rosie O'Grady.

Two blocks off Wall Street Rosie O'Grady Number two opened in 1973, the first bar in the area to offer Irish entertainment in that up-market area. Six or seven have followed since. "We did a big business in day trade with office people and I later bought the building. Earlier, I forgot to say, in 1971-2 I ran the Fordham Hill Steakhouse in the Bronx. I kept it just for two years.

"Manhattan's neighbourhoods are changing and improving in all directions, even up to 125th Street. The first midtown Rosie O'Grady's opened in 1977 at 51st Street, where we had a lease on a hotel premises. The owners were Equitable Life and they decided to build themselves, so they bought out the two remaining years of the lease from me for $1.5 million plus other incentives. One of the incentives was an option on restaurant space in the new building. We haven't yet taken up that option.

"So Rosie O'Grady's mid-town restaurant needed a nearby home, and we found it on 52nd Street where there was a Chinese restaurant with a 99-year lease. The rental was 5 per cent of the assessed value of the property, which was assessed at $500,000 for tax purposes. That was never the true value.

"The Chinese owners had 23 years gone on their 99-year lease, and they sold us the air rights. We now collect $45,000 a year for the air rights and we pay $25,000 in property taxes.

"It was the deal of the century", says Mike Carty proudly, "and we did it without benefit of lawyer and only lost three days' business".

In 1976, Mike bought Paddy Punch's of Punch's Cross in Limerick City. His third partner there, who runs the business, is Des O'Shea, brother of Cathal O'Shea, a well-known Dublin journalist on Tony O'Reilly's *Sunday World*, and son of Tim O'Shea who spent a lifetime on O'Reilly's *Evening Herald*. Des O'Shea's sister Deirdre now works in Rosie O'Grady's on Murray Street. Paddy Punch's has won numerous national awards for best pub and best pub grub.

Mike Carty is married to the former Angie Mulligan of Moyne, Co, Longford, whom he met in New York when she worked for Citibank. Now she works as a registered nurse. They have two children. Michael, who is 17, is at Fordham Prep. His father says he will be a commercial artist, architect or engineer. It is too early to say what Carolyn, now 14 and at Cardinal Spellman High, will do in life.

Mike goes to Ireland a couple of times a year, and in the summer the whole family goes. He has a deep interest in Gaelic games and has played for and managed the Leitrim football team in New York. He is also a member of the New York Roadrunners' Club and has run in both the London and New York marathons until a recent back operation removed a disc.

"A very Irish Club" to which he belongs is the New York Athletic Club. This is where his fellow New York restaurateur Jimmy Neary of Neary's got his first job when he arrived in America from Tubbercurry, Co. Sligo, Jimmy started as a towel boy and now that he has made good he has become the only former employee of the N.Y.A.C. ever accepted for membership.

Mike Carty is not active in any of the many Irish organisations in the United States, though he says that bar owners have to give financial support to every cause. "It's a built-in part of your budget". His children feel especially Irish. "The younger generation of Irish Americans are more aware of their identity than we were 20 years ago. As America gets older, it gets more ethnic. Not just the Irish—all hyphenates".

He attributes his singular success to his parents. "People put it down to luck", he says, "but the people I've met were people who hustled and worked and initiated. If you're the type of person who works hard, you will make it, though I admit there is an element of luck too.

"Any success I have I attribute to my parents. They laid down the values. We didn't have much when we were growing up but we did have their principles. It was a simple life but a great upbringing. My children may have more, but in a sense they can't have more".

JAMES A. DELANEY

THE newest star in the firmament of Irish America is a six-foot six-inches tall Texan called James A. Delaney, President of the Rand Development Corporation and National Chairman of the Irish American Unity Conference. This John Wayne lookalike with the slow easy smile and piercing pale-blue eyes has set the scene alight with his seeming contradictions, his charismatic influence and his meteoric rise to prominence, in Ireland as in America.

Five years ago the question; "Who is Jim Delaney?" would have been answered "Nobody". Now, while the question is still being asked, the answers are positive and if not always accurate, at least decorated with detail. Is he as rich as they say? Does he support Irish Northern Aid? Why does he not use the structures of the Irish State to promote economic development? The response to these queries must be to ask him.

But with Jim Delaney, as with most people, the best way to explain the man is by beginning at the beginning. He is not from Texas, but was born on the south side of Chicago in the Illinois Central Hospital in 1930. His mother was of German Wisconsin stock and his father was from Michigan. His grandfather, Peter Delaney, was from County Sligo, and he married Hannah Byron of Nenagh, County Tipperary, where in 1978 Jim Delaney met a cousin, Enda Morrison.

Delaney, who had a brother and two sisters, went to St. Cyril's Grammar School and then, across the street, to Mount Carmel High. At the University of Illinois he spent a year on an athletic scholarship without earning "one single academic credit". Already he was a useful boxer, first in the Irish neighbourhoods of Chicago, where he won the Golden Gloves in the tournament that brings together all the country's best boxers; then in the Marine Corps. He trained with the Police Athletic League and after his military service was awarded the Golden Gloves again in St. Mary's University in San Antonio, Texas. He also played basketball for St. Mary's and the University of Illinois.

In the Marines, he wore naval insignia when he served with an engineering battalion in Korea from 1951 to 1953. He was a navy medical corpsman third class with the Hospital Corps and his main duty was to find mines in front of the infantry. After the war he went to San Antonio, where as a much more mature student he studied philosophy, completing a four-year course in 2½ years and maintaining his interest in boxing and the Golden Gloves.

For a year after college, Jim Delaney worked as a research chemist for U.S. Steel, which had advertised in the *Chicago Tribune* for a paint chemist. Chemistry was his second worst subject, but he read up on the chemistry of paint the night before and got the job.

For no special reason except that he had always wanted to do it, he went to Europe for three months in 1956, making his first visit to Ireland and finding that the most helpful and friendly people were there and in England, Germany and Switzerland (a case of the end justifying the genes?).

The call of Texas was strong and Delaney went to Dallas to work as a medical representative for Ross Laboratories. The job entailed a month's training in headquarters in Columbus, Ohio, where one day in the Athletic Club he overheard a conversation about a decision to fire his boss. The man was only 42, and Delaney was so disgusted at this casual ending of a career that he decided never to go into industry.

In 1957 he established his own wholesale pharmaceutical processing firm. It was the beginning of the generic drug market and he did very well for 2½ years until a dispute arose over tetracyclene imported from Italy at 8 cents and selling as Noracyclene at 33 cents.

It was after that episode that the present Rand Development Corporation began in San Antonio as a real estate development firm.

With borrowed money Delaney bought an old department store scarred with broken windows and filled with dead pigeons. Within three months he had filled it with tenants. It was renamed the Rand Building and two of the eight floors were taken by the Government. The building, which is still in use, was the only premises in the city that was fully occupied for seven years.

In 1971 he bought El Tropicana, a 350-room hotel doing no business and badly in need of customers. To fill the rooms he called on the local military bases and then decided that his aim was to have the best conference hotel in San Antonio. He doubled the business and trebled the cash flow and in two years he had 40% of all the convention delegates in San Antonio, now a city of 875,000 people which has put it above Baltimore in size. He was named San Antonio Irishman of the Year in 1974.

Selling off both the Rand Building and the Tropicana in 1976, Jim

Delaney took a year off to give some help to the Incarnate Word High School and the Holy Spirit School and to work with the mayor on an urban renewal project called Centro 21, appointed by the City Council to revitalise downtown San Antonio.

The following year, when he had become President of the San Antonio Hotel Association, he bought a construction company that was owned by Maynard Braden, an old college friend. The marriage of Delaney's cash and Braden's talent resulted in joint ventures with financial institutions.

"And then", says Delaney, "it exploded. Apartments, office centres, shopping malls. At one time we had 22 operations going in San Antonio, Dallas, Wisconsin, California and Florida".

In the meantime, he invested in the manufacture of luggage and running shoes, as well as in retail stores, always taking at least 51% of the equity, usually 75-80%. These enterprises employ close to 300 people, while Rand Development has 110.

Millionaires, if they are not a dime a dozen are common enough in America. Independent estimates put Delaney's wealth at $40 to $50 million and certainly he has been in a position to be very generous with many Irish people and organisations who have sought his support.

About 1972, Jim Delaney joined the Harp and Shamrock Society, but it was not until he became a member of the Ancient Order of Hibernians in 1981 that he began to articulate his views on Ireland and the Irish Question. His attitude hardened with the death of Bobby Sands on hunger strike and the shooting of 12-year old Carol Ann Kelly by a British soldier using a plastic bullet.

He became a national director of the Ancient Order of Hibernians in 1982 when the Order's convention was hosted by San Antonio and Delaney. He has also been a member of the Irish American Cultural Institute for 10 years and a director since 1983, and he is a member of the American Irish Foundation.

From the National Convention of the A.O.H. in 1982, Jim Delaney derived the concept of founding the Irish American Unity Conference to form an umbrella organisation for the proliferation of 617 Irish American groups with a combined membership estimated at 1.2 million. He could see that there were bright, successful, interested people who could be brought together to realise the potential that there was in exerting Irish American influence.

Keeping in touch with these people, Delaney called a meeting in New York in January 1983, out of which came the assembly in Chicago in July that launched the Irish American Unity Conference. The conference issued a Manifesto and Program that said *inter alia:* "We believe that the British-generated Ulster problem is a danger to the Anglo-American alliance" and proclaimed its support for American legislation that would facilitate Irish national and economic development.

British withdrawal from Northern Ireland was to be completed in 2½ years, and the conference took positions on U.S. military and economic assistance to Britain; the outlawing of plastic bullets; a special U.S. envoy to the North, and support for the Ad Hoc Congressional Committee for Irish Affairs and the Friends of Ireland in Congress.

It was heady stuff, and there was more. Special emphasis was placed on economic development, the despatch of a fact-finding group to Ireland in October, 1983, and the "organisation of an investment banking group that will provide the necessary technical assistance to Irish industry".

The I.A.U.C. now claims to have 46,000 members and to be recruiting at the rate of 900 a week. That it is no flash in the pan is demonstrated by its high level of activity since Chicago. In April, 1984, there was an I.A.U.C. meeting in Washington, where Delaney told the Washington correspondent of *The Irish Times*: "There's room in this organisation for every view, for without every view there is no need to consider any view".

Six weeks later, an international economic development conference was sponsored by the I.A.U.C. and St. Mary's University, Delaney's *alma mater*. The theme of the meeting was "Freeing the Free Enterprise System: Ireland—A Case Study", and the keynote address was given by Dr. Ivor Kenny, Chancellor of the International Academy of Management and Senior Research Fellow at University College, Dublin. Dr Kenny was named Economist of the Year by the I.A.U.C. an award which included a $10,000 gift and was made by Jim Delaney as Chairman.

Among the members of the panels who contributed were the Rev. Harry Bohan, founder of the Rural Housing Organisation in the West of Ireland—"free enterprise at its best", as Delaney says; Tom Coffey, the award-winning playwright who is Director of Resource Development for Merck, Sharp and Dohme in Rahway, New Jersey; and Emmett O'Connell, managing director and founder of Eglinton Oil and Gas and a partner with Jim Delaney in Texas Continental Securities (T.C.S.).

T.C.S. is the practical expression of the Manifesto's demand for an investment banking group. It has offices in Harcourt Street, Dublin, and plans to use investors' money to buy up at least 51% of suitable Irish companies. At his press conference in Dublin in October, 1983, Delaney announced that he and his colleagues had $200 million to invest in the first year for the development of the Irish economy, but a prudent revision of that target was evidently made, whether for lack of suitable enterprises in which to invest or because the necessary money was not forthcoming, or both.

Delaney has a high regard for the New Ireland Forum Report. "I'm intrigued by the concept of federal or confederal co-operation such as there is between Texas and Oklahoma", he says. "But neither the Republic nor the North has a viable economy. If you remove the impediments to unity, how they unify is the business of the people of Ireland. It is very arrogant to try to force a political solution from outside (including Britain)....

"Yes, I have changed the emphasis of my thinking since the Manifesto. Michael Flannery (founder of Irish Northern Aid) has a different position from mine. I think history may prove him right. I'd like to see unity because it makes sense economically, culturally and socially.

"The North's is a story of subventions, industrial collapse and the flight of capital, all leading to the political instability of the whole island. Historical forces are inexorably forcing unity. In America, we're not sufficiently aware of the fact that the solution is the Irish people's business. We're being undermined here by the stress laid on violence by the Irish Government when they should be talking about the growth of tourism and the development of industry".

"Who is raising the spectre of violence? The Taoiseach, Dr FitzGerald, is talking about the need to prevent 2,000 people from contributing to violence; we're talking about 42 million Irish Americans who want to see progress on other fronts.

"I refuse to be intimidated by innuendo or rumour about what Noraid is all about. I'll publicly denounce that organisation as a fraud if they produce a scintilla of evidence.

"I'd be just as violently against the I.R.A. as you would be. I support the principle of self-defence, not shooting British soldiers and R.U.C. men. I don't see how any American can give blanket endorsement to the I.R.A. any more than I would give it to the U.S. military. We were wrong on the Falklands issue. Propping up the British invasion was against the Monroe Doctrine.

"You'd have to define for me what the I.R.A. is—the defence of homes or the commandeering of cars to blow up buildings".

Seán Cronin of *The Irish Times* bureau in Washington has summed Delaney up thus: "If you have the impression that Jim Delaney is a wild-eyed radical or a liberal humanitarian of some kind, you are wrong. In his own words he is 'a conservative Republican' which is how President Ronald Reagan describes himself".

The Irish Government has adopted an arms-length posture on Delaney. It believes that the I.A.U.C. launch was stage-managed by Noraid in order to gain Delaney's support, and it feels that its own agency, the Industrial Development Authority, is the logical source of advice and guidance on viable projects that the I.A.U.C. or T.C.S. might want to invest in.

Contradictions abound. The Chicago Manifesto urged co-operation with the Friends of Ireland group in Congress. Delaney is said to have no faith in the Friends of Ireland. He is quoted by Seán Cronin as saying:-

"I'm impressed by results and I don't see any. Nobody has made a serious effort to tap the enormous goodwill that exists in America for Ireland. You won't get it by going to Ted Kennedy, Pat Moynihan or Tip O'Neill...there are only two things that count in Washington, and you had better have one or the other—votes and money. We have both".

Jim Delaney the family man was speaking in an interview with the *San Antonio Express* when he said: "I don't support the I.R.A. But I have a 12 year-old daughter. If we lived in Ireland and they carried my daughter home with a British plastic bullet in her head and her only crime had been going to the store to get a carton of milk, I'd sure join the I.R.A. And if there wasn't one, I'd start one".

The daughter in question is Kathleen, who goes to the Holy Spirit Grammar School. She is one of three daughters of Jim and his wife Catherine, née Gleeson, who comes from County Tipperary grandparents, Caseys and Ryans ("that makes my children more Irish than I am", he says with a certain pride.) The oldest is Jean, who is 17 and a student at the Incarnate Word High School; and the youngest is Mary—"Mad Mary, Contrary Mary", he calls her with affection. She is five and at Coker Methodist School.

A particular friend of this family is Tomás Cardinal Ó Fiaich, Archbishop of Armagh and Primate of All Ireland. Cardinal Ó Fiaich stayed with the Delaneys in February, 1983, and got help from Delaney not only in raising $15,000 for the New University of Ulster at Coleraine, but earlier with the collecting of $100,000 for the library at St. Patrick's College, Maynooth.

If money talks, Jim Delaney may realise his dream of giving Irish America a united voice.

JOHN G. DRISCOLL

THE Irish Christian Brothers have only one University in the world, and its President is Brother John G. Driscoll, C.F.C. Soft of voice, easy of access, silver-haired and blue-eyed, Brother Driscoll presides over Iona College, New Rochelle, New York, which in his 14 years of office he has transformed from a small-town liberal arts institution into a centre for the new sciences and technologies.

By September, 1984, the new Murphy Science and Technology Center had emerged as "an ongoing working environment capable of acting as a powerful transmitter of both appropriate technological values and modern scientific and computer concepts".

In 1979, Brother Driscoll began to revise the undergraduate curriculum to integrate the liberal arts programme with a programme of technology. The Murphy Center is named after Joseph M. Murphy, President of Drexel Burnham Lambert Realty, who gave the naming gift of $1 million because, as he says, "I was so deeply indebted to the Christian Brothers for my education at Rice High School and as a scholarship student at Iona".

But Iona is going further than developing technological and scientific studies: it has spent money and teacher resources on the growth of a new core curriculum under which all students are required to take courses in three areas seen by the staff as critical: computer knowledge; reasoning and problem-solving, and communications skills. "What we believe", says Jack Driscoll, "is that the ordinary American college has to be able to do this. We are leagues ahead of big universities. It's hard to get recognised when you're poor. Everyone is looking to the biggies to lead the change. But IBM didn't invent the computer. Xerox didn't invent the photocopier. These were usually done by small hungry people who worked very hard and with passion. They usually don't wear three-piece suits".

There are now 200 personal computers for student use and another 100 for teaching staff and administration. Early in 1984, Iona was one of 15 colleges and universities, including MIT and Columbia and Stanford Universities, chosen to take part in an inter-university consortium on educational computing, the aim being to develop and test computer software to be used in the teaching of all academic disciplines. So recognition is coming to Iona, albeit slowly.

One of Brother Driscoll's objectives in 1971 was to build the college's basketball team into a national power. By 1980 the Iona Gaels ranked as high as 19th in the nation; had twice got into the National Collegiate Athletic Association tournament, and improved their record to 29 victories and five losses compared with 16 losses and four wins in the 1978 season. No longer do people in basketball discussions say: "Iona who?".

Like many smaller community colleges, Iona suffers from the perception that it attracts only students who could not get into the senior universities. Its students reply by pointing out its outstanding qualities: it is small (it still has an enrolment of only 6,000 students); there is a friendly atmosphere on the campus; its faculty members are accessible and willing to work with students, and it has an expanding computer science department.

Most of the students come from within 50 miles away, "the sons and daughters of the first generation". A large number work their way through college, and while most take jobs directly after they graduate, others are accepted into the graduate schools of Ivy League universities.

Iona was founded in 1940 by the Irish Christian Brothers. It had 93 students in its first year; now its student numbers are double what they were in 1972 when Jack Driscoll took the helm, and the academic staff is up from 197 to 342. Millions have been spent on the 55-acre campus and the annual budget is $27 million. As well as the Murphy Science and Technology Center, a new Mulcahy Center with a 3,500-seat gymnasium has been added to the facilities. The donor is John A. Mulcahy of Waterville, County Kerry, a benefactor whose name is writ large on the map of modern Ireland. Not for nothing has Brother Driscoll become "Iona's finest salesman", to quote a colleague.

An important test of the quality of an academic institution is how it relates to its immediate environment. Town and gown do not always harmonise, and with this thought in mind Brother Driscoll has evolved, with Sister Dorothy Ann Kelly, the President of the College of New Rochelle, a "College as Citizen" programme which allows the colleges to act as think-tanks and resource centres for the city while Iona and New Rochelle students are permitted to gain work experience in municipal departments.

"The college can't survive unless the city does", Brother Driscoll says. "We want to make the two colleges an important resource to the community. We'd like to think of ourselves as good citizens". It was as a good citizen that Jack Driscoll was recently appointed Chairman of the Westchester Public Utility Agency, where he can use his technological literacy to find solutions to complex community problems. National and state committees and academic boards on which he serves recognise the qualities of this "Christian Brother who happens to be a college president", as he describes himself. He is now no stranger to the corridors of power in Albany and Washington where, with his colleagues in other colleges, he states the case for the independent sector in higher education.

In 1983, President Driscoll took a look at himself, America and the world, and decided to take a six-month sabbatical tour, "an extraordinary opportunity", he said at the time, "for personal renewal and professional growth". Extraordinary it was, with two months in Europe; two in Southeast Asia, and two in the Eastern Mediterranean. What he found surprised and sometimes shocked him, and he has been fearless in sharing his experiences with audiences of staff, students, parents and governors.

"I will never be the same person I was before the journey", he says. "I keep going over in my mind that we are involved right now in defining what it means to be an American at this particular time in history, and the responsibility we have in serving humanity. America's foreign policy is too far removed from most of the American people. We have let too much decision-making go out of our own hands. Consequently we are becoming less democratic than we should be.

"We are supporting actions in several countries that we should never support or allow. And these violations of human rights, with the support of our weapons and blessings, are not only embarrassing but positively frightening.

"We are going to have to learn to deal in a world where our superior weapons no longer defend us. We must learn to defend ourselves through peace and justice, not through weapons. It's going to be a tough lesson to swallow. After all, we were brought up on the John Wayne syndrome.

"We have become so intellectual that we forget the role the heart should play in our lives. We are not training the heart for compassion".

But in all the poverty, he found pride. "These people are determined that one day soon they will compete on an equal footing with the developed countries. They no longer fear us. The attack on the Marine base in Lebanon proved that.

"I didn't understand up to now that God is using these people, the poor who are the Chosen People of the New Testament, to challenge me so that I can be saved. With so many imprisoned and thirsty the only question in the end is: When I was hungry, did you give me to eat?

"We're going to be asked about the talents. The only wrong answer is to say: 'I buried them'. Mother Teresa in Calcutta, living with 247 novices in that one convent, repeated to me what she said at our Commencement at Iona several years ago: 'You cannot do what I do, and I cannot do what you do. But together we do something beautiful for God'.

"I don't know enough about the poor. I spent a long time talking to them and about them. I did so with His Holiness the Dalai Lama. (He had sent word to me that I should come wearing the jeans that I was travelling in, rather than a black clerical suit, because, he said: 'There are already enough things that divide us'.) He spoke about the need for compassion and the training of the heart. Western monks and nuns had learned much about health and education while Eastern monks had learned much about prayer, he said, and it was time that we exchanged what we had learnt".

The Dalai Lama is due to follow Mother Teresa to Iona College in October, 1984, six months after Brother Driscoll returned after journeying 28,000 miles through 22 countries.

One of the countries that Jack Driscoll visited was Ireland, birthplace of both his parents. He comes of "100% Kerry stock", his mother having been from Ballydavid, near Dingle, and his father from Lauragh, "well out from Kenmare on the Kerry side of the Tim Healy Pass".

His father, who is 78 now, was 19 when he emigrated and worked as a labourer on the railway express. His aunt was already in New York, and his older brother also preceded him. Jack Driscoll's mother went to an uncle in Springfield, Massachusetts, who sent for his nieces one by one. She began her new life as a housemaid and came to New York, where she met her future husband at one of the many Irish ballrooms and social clubs that littered the Irish neighbourhoods of the city.

Jack Driscoll was born in La Salle Street, near Amsterdam Avenue and 124th Street. Jack is the oldest of four. His brother Michael is a Christian Brother in Chicago; his sister Geraldine is married, and his younger brother Kevin is pension and benefit manager for the Steamfitters' Union in New York City.

His first visit home in 1971 opened his eyes to his own nature and personality. "It was more moving than any retreat", he says. "The parts from which my parents came were relatively undisturbed by progress and I saw almost precisely what my father had left. The attitudes and values were probably very much the same and my people had not opted to have electricity so there was not even television.

"The conversation in the pub at night was very much as it always had been. It showed a community discernment that still is not that much changed. It may be endangered by TV, but still...

"I felt: 'That's where I could have been born. These people are very much like me'. None of them had very much formal education, so I had to face the fact that some of these people were brighter than I am. Brosnans, Kellehers, O'Donnells . . . . . they are natively brighter".

Jack Driscoll's mother was dead, so it was his father and he who made the journey. "Several times during those summer evenings, as I sat alone in their Kerry homelands, I learned more about my mother and father than I ever could have if we had never left New York. What courage and faith, heartache and fright must have tumbled inside them on those emigrant ships...Who cried harder and longer: the son and daughter going down the road, suitcase in hand, or the mother and father seeing the last of a loved child?"

He talks of hiring a car from Dan Dooley's Rent-A-Car at Shannon Airport. Dooley's agent set about completing the forms.

"Well now, Father", he began. "Excuse me", I said, "I am a Christian Brother". "Oh, you're a teacher then?" "Yes I am", I replied. "Elementary or the secondary?" he asked. "Neither", said I, "I'm in a university". "Oh isn't that wonderful, Brother?" he said. "I've had very little schooling myself, Brother, but I have great respect for it. I'll say this to you, and I mean every word of it: without an education, you have to use your brains to get along in this world".

Brother Driscoll's own education began at St. Joseph's Parish School on 125th Street. Then he went to St. Rose of Lima elementary, run by the Dominican nuns. The Christian Brothers at All Hallows in the Bronx gave him his early secondary education and then at 15 he joined them, and was trained at West Park, New York, about 90 miles from the city on the Hudson River.

"In the 1940s, it was acceptable to adjust and enjoy. I had my parents' support and at that time West Park was the only house of formation for North America and Canada".

Brother Driscoll, who is known simply as "Brother" to thousands of students and staff, is a graduate of the Iona College class of 1954. He got a doctorate in mathematics from Columbia University and returned to his *alma mater* in 1965 to teach mathematics.

Four years later the Board of Trustees began the search for the sixth president of the college. His name was put forward, but others felt that at 37 he was too young and lacked administrative experience. His advocates pressed their case: he possessed a rare combination of warmth, energy, intelligence and vision, and these qualities would compensate for whatever he lacked in experience. His name was put on the panel, the Board interviewed him, and the Board was captivated. He wanted to transform Iona, to put it on a par with schools three or four times its age. "That group of trustees", says Brother Richard DeMaria, the college's executive vice-president, "was only the first of many boards to be challenged and enthused by the vision and aura of John Driscoll".

A former member of the Board of Trustees recalls: "Almost immediately the students sensed that they had a leader whose idealism not only greatly exceeded theirs, but was vastly deeper and more soundly based. The rapport which he had always had with his students quickly generated a spurt of confidence, even trust, replacing the then distrust of anyone over 35, especially anyone in a position of authority or responsibility. This was the first noticeable contribution and for many faculty members and even more parents, the most welcome".

The growth of Iona College has taken several forms. It has grown in area, in buildings, in equipment, in numbers and in curricula. But most of all, under Brother Driscoll's direction and that of the hundreds of men and women who form the Iona community, it has grown in reputation to become for the New World what its famous predecessor under Columba became in the sixth century, a "light of learning and piety".

JACK DUNFEY

THE Dunfey saga is remarkable by any yardstick. From the town of Lowell, Massachusetts, came a family of eight boys and four girls, all of them surviving and five of them destined, with their mother, to create a chain of thirty distinctive hotels that now covers two continents.

John Dunfey, known to his friends as Jack, emerged by common consent as the leader of this family enterprise whose origins lie in the variety store operated by Leroy W. Dunfey and his wife, Catherine Manning Dunfey. Leroy Dunfey died in 1952 at the age of 60, but Catherine, who left elementary school at 12 to work in the mill at Lowell, lived until 1982 and encouraged five of her sons—Jack, Jerry, Walter, Bob and Bill—to take the plunge into hotel-keeping in 1954, when they bought Lamie's Tavern, a small country inn, in Hampton, New Hampshire.

Catherine Dunfey, going on 60 at the time, became Chairman of the Board, and Jack was President and Chief Executive Officer. They enlarged Lamie's and gave it what came to be known as the Dunfey touch—early American furniture, big fireplaces, dark oak tables and pictures of ships.

Soon this third-generation Irish family was, in the words of a contemporary reporter, "poking about the New England countryside buying up one hotel after another", and with the acquisition of eleven hotels was grossing $15 million by 1969.

That was the year in which another watershed was reached. The chain up to then was mainly rural, mainly of the motor hotel type. When the family decided to buy the famous but bankrupt Parker House in Boston, they moved into the senior league, acquiring their first large hotel in a large city, a hotel, moreover, that is the oldest continuously operated hotel in the United States.

The Dunfey story twists again in 1971, when the need to inject more capital caused the group to merge with Aetna Life and Casualty, the largest financial services company in the U.S. with assets of $47 billion. Although the chain was now 100% owned by Aetna, the five brothers, soon to be joined by a sixth, Roy, stayed on as the executive management team.

Four years later, new regulations compelled insurance companies to divest themselves of non-insurance activities and with Morgan Guaranty Bank acting as brokers, the 14 hotels—plus another seven which were under management contract—were acquired by the Irish national airline, Aer Lingus, as part of its programme of concentric diversification. Negotiations took over a year but on January 1st, 1976, Aer Lingus, under its Chief Executive—Ancillary Activities, Gerald P. Dempsey, took 100% of the equity in Dunfey Hotels at a cost to Aer Lingus of $750,000.

Now an international group, Dunfeys had Gerry Dempsey as Chairman and Jack Dunfey as Chief Executive Officer on a five-year contract. This was later extended to eight as the group developed further under Aer Lingus ownership. On April 1st, 1983, Jon Canas took up the executive role and Jack Dunfey, who had been working since the age of seven and has now turned 60, became Vice-Chairman. His five brothers still remain interested in various areas of the company's activities and though Jon Canas operates out of New York, Jack keeps his headquarters in Lamie's Tavern and cherishes the extra time he can give to his broad range of other interests.

This quite unusual company, linking as it does a family in the United States with a State-owned institution in Ireland, has prospered greatly from the unique diversity of its inputs. Soon after Jack Dunfey's retirement from active executive duties, the company acquired a small but significant business, the Omni International Hotel Corporation. This marriage, initiated by Jack Dunfey, was consummated in January, 1984, and clearly is the harbinger of great things to come.

With the traditional inn-keeping style of the Dunfeys, the support of Aer Lingus and now the new thrust of the Omni name, this company is setting its corporate sights higher than may ever have been dreamed about back in 1954.

Jack Dunfey is also a director, as is his brother Walter, of the Ireland Fund which is chaired by Tony O'Reilly. In 1974, Jack and his brothers founded the New England Circle to "assemble for the discussion of social, political, literary and educational topics; to exchange ideas and opinions that can lead to constructive change in our lives, in our nation, and throughout the world".

The discussions, more than 40 of them to date, are always held in the Parker House, Boston, which in the heart of a Dunfey must take pride of place as the flagship of the chain although perhaps strictly speaking the Berkshire Place in New York can claim that honour.

(Among the discussion leaders are many household names, including Boston's native son, Senator Edward Kennedy; the writer and columnist Jimmy Breslin; Mayor Andrew Young of Atlanta, Georgia; Coretta Scott King, widow of the Rev. Martin Luther King, and herself a human rights activist; Speaker Thomas P. "Tip" O'Neill; the economist J. K. Galbraith; John Hume, leader of Northern Ireland's Social Democratic and Labour Party; New York's Mayor Edward Koch; Ambassador Henry Cabot Lodge; Ralph Nader, the consumer advocate; Jane Fonda, Robert McNamara and Bianca Jagger.)

A memorable dinner to mark Jack Dunfey's retirement was held in the Parker House in October, 1983, a tribute, as the menu card said, "to people, ideas, education, peace and Jack Dunfey". The master of ceremonies was Senator Kennedy; the programme director was Judge David S. Nelson of the United States District Court; grace was said by Monsignor Philip J. Kenny and, after the recipient charities had been acknowledged by Mayor Young, there were some words from Jon Canas, Gerry Dempsey, Coretta Scott King, and Jack himself, a former World War II pilot. The inscription by John Gillespie Magee Jr. speaks for itself:

Sunward I've climbed and joined the tumbling mirth
Of sun-split clouds—and done a thousand things....

Another and a major interest of Jack Dunfey's is the establishment of the U.S. Peace Academy. He was appointed in 1979 by the U.S. Senate to be a member of the U.S. Commission on Proposals for the National Academy of Peace and Conflict Resolution to conduct, under its Chairman, Senator Spark Matsunaga of Hawaii, a two-year study which was presented as a final report to President Reagan in October, 1981. One of Jack Dunfey's fondest hopes became a reality in October, 1984, when the Peace Academy was formally established by Congress.

"Half of my travel nowadays is personal", says this far-from-retired campaigner whose work for the famine relief agency Oxfam carried him to Grenada in April, 1984, "to see the results of the invasion", and to Bermuda the following month for a two-day seminar on devising a five-year plan for the Ireland Fund.

The Dunfeys have always been close to the Kennedy family. Bill Dunfey worked for two years for John F. Kennedy before the 1960 victory and was active in Robert F. Kennedy's later campaigns. At their annual Christmas Board meetings in the old days, when the family shared out the proceeds of the business, individual members were docked for the time they had spent on politics during the previous 12 months. "I'm still wounded", Bill is quoted as having said, "from the years I spent with Jack Kennedy".

Only Jack Dunfey concentrated totally on the hotel business. But Edward Kennedy has been a long-time friend and sailing companion and in the past year or so, the two have become closer. In January, 1984, Jack had dinner with the Senator and his mother, Rose, in her Palm Beach house. He found the 94-year-old lady "failing physically but mentally amazingly alert. Ted does a great job with her", he says admiringly. It was this firm friendship that resulted in the raising of $150,000 for charity at the Boston dinner in 1983 at which Senator Kennedy acted as master of ceremonies.

That dinner, as well as every New England Circle meeting for the past ten years, was held in the Parker House, which has always acted as host to famous guests, presidents and kings, politicians, actors and above all, perhaps, literary men.

Harvey Parker, like the Dunfey family after him, was born far enough from the patrician preserves of Beacon Hill to confound anyone who might have predicted that his name would one day be a household word in Boston. He was born in 1805 in the village of Temple, Maine (then in the Commonwealth of Massachusetts). He was 20 when he left home for Boston with a few clothes and less than a dollar. Yet by 1832, he had gathered together $432, enough to buy an eating house which he promptly signed "Parker's Restaurant".

On Monday, October 8th, 1855, the *Boston Transcript* announced the opening of the Parker House, "this elegant new hotel" whose French chef, Sanzian, was reported around the town to be getting the astounding salary of $5,000 a year at a time when a good chef could be hired for eight dollars a week. Boston cream and lemon meringue pies become gourmet food under his direction and William Makepeace Thackeray contended that a plump Wellfleet oyster at Parker's made him feel as if he were swallowing a baby. This remark was taken to be a compliment.

Most of the hotel's waiters were Irish. As the *Boston Globe* put it: "They made the service at Parker's the best possible and knew the tastes of their patrons who often said they found a more agreeable home at Parker's than at any other hotel. The head waiters were invariably Irish".

For academics, as for shipping merchants and traders, the atmosphere of the bar was found to be convivial and caused the humorist, Artemus Ward, to aver that "Harvard University is pleasantly and conveniently situated in the bar-room of Parker's in School street". Proper Bostonians felt at home at the Parker House, with its grace and good taste, its regard for form and manners, its dignity and solemnity.

As its reputation grew, the Parker House became the fasionable place for the celebrities of the day, such as Edwin Booth, brother of John Wilkes Booth; Henry Irving, Ellen Terry and Sarah Bernhardt. In April, 1865, only eight days before John Wilkes Booth made his assassin's appearance on the stage of Ford's Theatre in Washington, D.C. and shot President Abraham Lincoln, he had stayed at Parker's. It was a visit of which Harvey Parker was not especially proud.

Early in the history of the Parker House, the Saturday Club was born. In 1857, its members made a significant contribution to literature when they published the first issue of the distinguished *Atlantic Monthly*, its editor being James Russell Lowell. Ralph Waldo Emerson, the philosopher, and the other founding members were soon joined by Dr. Oliver Wendell Holmes, the physician-poet, Nathaniel Hawthorne, the novelist, and two poets, Henry Wadsworth Longfellow and John Greenleaf Whittier.

They met in a private dining room upstairs, usually at three o'clock. Louis Agassiz, the scientist, sat at the head of the table; Longfellow, with his silver hair and beard, at the foot. Emerson sat near Longfellow, puffing the stub of a cigar, while Lowell, Whittier, Hawthorne, Holmes and Charles Francis Adams, son and grandson of Presidents, exchanged shafts of wit, gossip, criticism and philosophical thought.

The meal, usually of seven courses, was served by the Irish waiters who kept glasses refilled with sherry, sauternes, claret and sometimes a magnum of Moët.

By 1867, when Charles Dickens made his second visit to Boston, he found the hotel a curious mixture of styles and heights, but the Parker House was a comfortable place in which to plan his popular and highly rewarding lecture tour, rehearse his readings and rest between performances. "The cost of living", he wrote to his daughter, "is enormous, but happily we can afford it. I dine today with Longfellow, Emerson, Holmes and Agassiz". Parker's was Dickens' home-from-home during the whole of his five months' stay in the United States.

Later, Holmes penned a poem entitled "At the Saturday Club". It goes from bad to verse, but it is worth recording the last two lines of his reference to the Parker House:

Such guests! What famous names its record boasts,
Whose owners wander in the mob of ghosts!

Apart from an annex built in 1886, on which rests the hotel's claim to continuous operation, the Parker House was totally rebuilt in 1925 to the elegant designs of the architects Desmond and Lord. It enjoyed a new burst of prosperity between its opening in 1927 and the Wall Street Crash of 1929, but it was another 40 years before the dynamic Dunfeys restored it to its former glory, adding to its comfort and facilities but showing a proper regard for its proud place in the history of Boston.

Like Harvey Parker before him, Jack Dunfey and his brothers worked hard to create their own American dream. All 12 of the children did a stint in Leroy Dunfey's store, two at a time, between 5 a.m. and 2 a.m. each day. They started at the age of seven in an area known as "The Acre", which had been donated by the Church for Irish immigrants to settle in.

Jack's parents were born in the United States. He knows that his maternal grandmother, Mary O'Connor, married James Manning of Ballyferriter, near Dingle, Co. Kerry. His cousin, Denis O'Connor, in Ballyferriter, where Jack's brother Bob now has a holiday home, was a schoolteacher for 30 years and his father before him was master of the school for 40 years. Denis has written several books on the Dingle Peninsula and his sister, Catherine Manning Dunfey, never lost contact with the home place. "Through her", says Jack, "we developed our interest in Ireland and between 1968 and 1980, all 13 of us made several visits as a family. Twice we brought 40 Dunfeys with us".

It is on Leroy Dunfey's side of the family that more work has to be done, though we know that Leroy's father was Nicholas and his grandfather Matthew. Roy Dunfey recalls Eoin ("the Pope") O'Mahony's saying that "we were from Ossory, somewhere in Kilkenny", but "the Pope" O'Mahony, raconteur, wit and genealogist supreme, has left us this many a year.

Jack Dunfey was the third boy, the fifth child. He went to Keith Academy in Lowell, run by the Xaverian Brothers, and now defunct. He and all the others went in turn to the University of New Hampshire, where Jack majored in liberal arts.

Then came World War II and Jack became a pilot in the U.S. Air Force. (Bill and Paul were in the Marines) The end of the war was the beginning of the Dunfey dynasty. The five brothers started a seasonal fried-clam stand at Hampton Beach, a lively resort on the New

Hampshire coast. After four years they had a pizza parlor, a penny arcade, one big restaurant and three little ones.

It was still a big step to the purchase of Lamie's Tavern in 1954; a giant stride to ownership of the Parker House in 1969. Now six of the eight boys are in Dunfey Hotels. A seventh, Richard, is Chief Justice of the New Hampshire Superior Court and Paul still lives in Lowell where it all began. All of the four girls became nuns in the Order of Notre Dame de Namur, and all four have since left the religious life. Two are married, one engaged to be married. "It was", says Jack, "more a change of career than anything else; all of them have gone on to do other things than teaching. They have begun the second phase of their lives".

Jack himself is divorced and the father of four children. Susan, who spent a year at Hume Dudgeon's famous establishment at Burton Hall, Leopardstown, County Dublin, has a riding establishment in Rye, New Hampshrie. She is married. David is an attorney with a Boston law firm. Philip, who got himself married in May, 1984, is an independent mechanical contractor in Portsmouth, New Hampshire, and Stephen has just graduated in Political Science from his father's old university, the University of New Hampshire at Durham. At 19, Stephen was elected a State Representative—a Democrat in a Republican town—served two terms and became Assistant Minority Leader at 22.

The last word may safely be left to older brother Roy, who joined the founding five only 15 years ago and looks after employee relations: "I can talk a little bit more objectively", he says. "The one thing that impressed me was the way we all could complement each other and stand in for each other in any given situation. Some 27 years ago, we were 50 to 60 people of whom five happened to be Dunfeys. We want to maintain that kind of relationship in Dunfey Hotels, and you can't do it by lip service".

THOMAS W. GLEASON

"WHEN I was on national television in 1979 being asked why the International Longshoremen's Association was interfering in politics by refusing to load wheat shipments to Russia over the invasion of Afghanistan, the interviewer turned to me and said: 'And what about Red China?' 'Looks good on a white tablecloth', I answered, suddenly remembering a joke that my friend Hal Roach the Dublin comedian tells. Hal called me afterwards and said: 'Hey, I hear you're stealing my material!'"

The speaker is Thomas "Teddy" Gleason, President for the past 21 years of the International Longshoremen's Association, which has 116,000 members in Atlantic and Gulf coast ports, on the Great Lakes and major rivers, and in Puerto Rico and Canada. He was 83 years old on November 8, 1983, and, half-joking whole earnest, expects to live to be 103.

"While I was watching a belly-dancer on the Nile recently, a palm reader told me I would live to be 103. My house number is also 103. If there's a lonely hearts club in Ireland, you might tell the girls I'd be a good catch—I've only 20 years to live and I've got a good pension".

It would be a serious mistake to take Teddy Gleason's humour for the ramblings of an old man. He is in at his desk before 7 o'clock every morning, for two reasons. One, because his own life on the docks accustomed him to early rising, but more important, because with the three different time zones he has to contend with, he can deal instantly with any incipient wildcat strike anywhere by always being available on the telephone. Talk of retirement is dismissed: "They just elected me for four more years. I think the undertaker will get me before I leave the job".

On St. Patrick's Day, March 17th, 1984, Teddy Gleason acted as Grand Marshal of the New York Parade. He even did a little dance along the green-painted line as he led the march, and he recalled as he played his role all day long the warm letter he had earlier received from his good friend, President Ronald Reagan, who wrote in part: "Nancy and I are delighted to send our warmest congratulations and best wishes on your selection . . . . . This will be a thrilling moment for you, your family, and all the sons and daughters of Erin. I share your pride in our common Irish heritage and know what a meaningful occasion this is for you…".

On the previous St. Patrick's Day, 1983, Teddy Gleason was Grand Marshal of the Brooklyn Irish-American parade and thus he missed the controversy that surrounded the selection of I.R.A. veteran, Mike Flannery, as Grand Marshal of the New York parade, controversy that extended to an Irish Government boycott of the parade because, as one official of a State-sponsored company, Aer Lingus, put it, "the parade was hijacked by extremists". The 1983 parade, in spite or because of the trouble surrounding it, was reported to have been the most successful yet held.

Teddy Gleason's position on the Irish question is cautious. He says: "Forget about politics. Get unity first and we in America will do all we can to help". Yet, hanging on the wall of his office in 17 Battery Place, New York, is a framed handkerchief embroidered with the words: "From all the boys in Long Kesh, 1975". Long Kesh in Northern Ireland is officially known as the Maze prison and is where the IRA and INLA hunger strikers led by Bobby Sands died in 1981. So there is a certain ambivalence on the issue of the right to use physical force in Ireland, and Teddy Gleason is, understandably in the leader of a great labour union that embraces many ethnic groups and must support the Administration in some areas in order to win its backing in others, no different from most of the leaders of Irish America. But he does admire his co-eval Flannery and says the IRA would be heroes anywhere else.

"I like Reagan", he says. "I like what he's doing". And unequivocally Gleason has put the power of the longshoremen behind the President's re-election. "God be with the days", he recalls, "when if you didn't vote Democrat you weren't allowed to go to church on Sundays".

In 1969, Teddy Gleason was elected Vice-President of the Executive Council of the American Federation of Labor and Congress of Industrial Organisations (AFL-CIO) and he has been re-elected every two years ever since. Last year the AFL-CIO President Lane Kirkland expanded Gleason's role by making him Chairman of the International Affairs Committee. This dynamic and progressive labour leader has also since 1974 been a Vice President of the worldwide International Transport Workers' Federation which represents over six million transport workers in 78 countries.

Whatever the marks of a shrewd and talented negotiator, Teddy

Gleason has them. He is chiefly responsible—though it would be wrong to think of him as anything but *primus inter pares* with people like John Bowers, the ILA's Executive Vice-President—for the waterfront labour peace visible in all ILA ports in recent years. In his role as the union's principal negotiator, Gleason has significantly reversed the trend of labour unrest that had beset the docks for many years.

When he got to the top in 1963, the union was $1.5 million in the red. Within three years, it was solvent. "I never go to bed without saying the Rosary", Gleason will tell you. "And then I say: God bless those guys who pay their dues".

Through the publication of an ILA newspaper, *The Longshore News*, each port learned what the others were doing and a once-divided and embattled membership felt its morale rise.

Then came the landmark negotiations of 1964-65. A great deal of economic insecurity remained so long as the senior men could not be assured of an adequate income in the wake of automation. Seniority was finally recognised so that the old-timers could no longer be pushed aside to make way for younger men with stronger backs. Medical, welfare and clinical services were introduced.

Gleason's team was ready to accommodate to the reality of a new era in cargo handling. The main problem they foresaw was how to prevent containerisation from destroying the union, and what they achieved in 1964-65 was to benefit the membership for at least the next 20 years.

In April, 1965, a contract was arrived at. A gigantic breakthrough was made with the establishment of the Guaranteed Annual Income (G.A.I), a revolutionary feat which was acknowledged throughout the United States and the world. In return for certain concessions, including the size of the work gangs, management guaranteed 1,600 hours of work or pay for every man who had worked at least 700 hours in the previous contract year in the Port of New York. That meant that every docker was assured of 32 hours of work every week, so long as he presented himself for work. Philadelphia longshoremen were guaranteed 1,500 hours and in Boston and other major ports there were lesser terms. It was, with an 80 cents fringe benefit package in all ports, the best dock pact in history, though both John Bowers and Teddy Gleason accepted that it had its faults.

Pensioners now get up to $900 a month, including about 200 retired longshoremen living in Ireland in Arklow, Kinsale, Clare and Galway, whose Mayor gave Gleason a gift of a harp—no irony intended—when he visited the 500-year-old city at the time of his 83rd birthday. To enable him to get to Galway from Dublin, the famous showman/restaurateur Sean Kinsella of the Mirabeau lent Gleason his Rolls-Royce.

Gleason, who visits Ireland at least four times a year, plans to have an Irish reunion soon for the men retired around the Irish coast, but although he attended and spoke at the 1984 convention of the Irish Transport and General Workers' Union in Liberty Hall, Dublin, Ireland is far from being the only focus of his interest outside the United States. Indeed he was in Bremen, Germany, when the famous General Secretary of the ITGWU, Michael Mullen, died in Frankfurt. They had been friends for 30 years.

Throughout the 1960s and 1970s, while Teddy Gleason was vastly improving the wages and benefits of his members, he was also actively serving the cause of the AFL-CIO. The late President, George Meany, repeatedly called on him to represent the federation at international meetings and conventions. In 1967, Meany appointed Gleason a fraternal delegate to represent the 14 million members at the fifth national convention of the Vietnamese Confederation of Labour in Saigon and in 1969 he performed a similar service in Tel Aviv, Israel. Again in 1970 he represented the AFL-CIO at the annual conference of the British Trades Union Congress. He was in Israel again in 1974 and in Lima, Peru, in 1978.

The present President of the AFL-CIO, Lane Kirkland, has made similar demands on Teddy Gleason's stamina and time in order to put his international experience to work in trouble spots around the globe. In April, 1983, Gleason went to Paris and Cairo (where he met his first belly dancer) as part of an American delegation seeking a solution to the Lebanon problem.

Labour was not alone in calling on him for advice. President Lyndon B. Johnson got him to serve as a member of his Maritime Advisory Committee and in 1965 Secretary of State Dean Rusk asked him to investigate the movement of cargo in the Port of Saigon in order to recommend a programme to relieve congestion. He made four trips to South-East Asia at the union's expense and later did a similar study for the Port of Mombasa, Kenya. Scores of other Government, maritime and union officials have sought the counsel and leadership of this dogged veteran during the nearly seven decades that he has devoted to the longshore industry, not least President Reagan who, in 1982, appointed Gleason to his Administration's Maritime Advisory Committee.

Thomas William Gleason was born, the oldest of 13 children, on November 8, 1900, in a tenement neighbourhood of Greenwich Village, New York, not a mile from where he still lives. His father and grandfather, both dock workers, emigrated from Nenagh, County Tipperary, where they lived within an ass's roar of the church. His mother, Mary Quinn, was from Drumquin, near Omagh, County Tyrone, and came to America as cook with a rich family in Philadelphia. "All the Irish landed in Philadelphia in those days", recalls Teddy Gleason, who acquired that nickname as a child to distinguish him from his father and grandfather, both called Thomas.

At the age of 15 he went to work beside his father on the West Side piers in Manhatten, where conditions were so wretched on the docks that he resolved to do something to bring dignity and self-respect to the longshoremen. When he joined the ILA at the age of 19, he was one of the youngest fully-fledged dockers in New York. He worked in a number of jobs, checker, billing clerk, longshoreman, winch driver, truck loader, timekeeper and, by 1932, dock superintendent for Atlantic, Gulf and West Indies Lines, working from 7 a.m. to 5 p.m. for 35 cents an hour.

His steady rise came to an abrupt halt when stevedoring companies and steamship lines banded together to blacklist Teddy Gleason because of his increasing activity in organising the union. That is why, at the depth of the Great Depression and cut off from longshoring, he was compelled to take two jobs to support his wife and three children. By day, he pushed a handcart in a sugar factory and by night, working from 7 p.m. to 10 p.m., he sold frankfurters on a stand at Coney Island.

Two memories stand out, both sources of wry amusement to him now. One was of giving free frankfurters to his own children as though they were his to give ("When you eat pea soup six days a week, you have to pray to God for strength. My weight went down from 160 pounds to 128".) And the other was pushing his handcart on March 4th, 1933, and listening to the newly-inaugurated President Franklin D. Roosevelt say on the radio: "You have nothing to fear but fear itself". His reaction was to say to himself: "Gleason, keep pushing".

Drinking "Mr. Hennessy" brought his weight back to normal and he has never drunk anything but cognac. He never smoked either, nor did any of his family, except one sister. Eleven of the 13 are still alive.

President Roosevelt's New Deal brought the legal recognition of labour unions and Teddy Gleason was able to return to his work and his union organising. Soon he became President and Business Agent of Checkers' Local 1346 in the ILA, which eventually merged with three other locals to form Local 1, of which Gleason became President, a post he still holds after 26 years.

In 1953 he was elected general organiser of the International Longshoremen's Association and by 1961, he was Executive Vice President and Chief Negotiator with the waterfront employers. Two years later, he had reached the top and there he has stayed for 21 years, honoured by countless civic and fraternal organisations and sitting on a number of committees and executive boards.

At present he is on the Board of Directors of the African-American Labor Center and the American Institute for Free Labor Development. He sits on the Executive Councils of the Irish Institute, New York, and the American Irish Historical Society, which in 1980 made him a medalist, a distinction he shares with Ronald Reagan, two Governors of New York State and the late George Meany.

Teddy Gleason is a member of the Friendly Sons of St. Patrick and the 75,000-member Ancient Order of Hibernians which in 1982 presented him with its John F. Kennedy Memorial Award, given biennially to an Irish-American leader. Other organisations, such as the Irish National Caucus, the New York City Police Department Emerald Society, the United Irish Counties' Association, and the County Tipperary Association (the Nenagh connection) have honoured him likewise.

He is founder and co-chairman, with Bill Treacy of the Union of Operating Engineers, of the Irish-American Labor Coalition; and in June, 1982, he arranged a meeting in New York between the Irish Prime Minister, Charles J. Haughey, and leading American trades union leaders. Ways in which the labour movement in the United States might effectively assist in the resolution of conflict in Northern Ireland were explored and further meetings were planned.

Teddy Gleason holds the honorary degree of Doctor of Laws from Molloy College in Rockville Center, New York, which he received in 1980. He is a member of Epiphany Parish and says of the Archbishop, John O'Connor: "The Church needed a guy like him—he's street-wise and has the gift of the gab".

Gleason's wife, who was born Emma Martin, died in 1961. His oldest son, Thomas Jr., practices law and is general counsel to the ILA. The middle son, John, is in the mortgage business, and Robert works with the ILA. All but two of his 14 grandchildren have been to Ireland; and now there are two great-grandchildren waiting to learn of their roots at first hand.

On Teddy Gleason's tidy desk there is a plaque that reads: "When I'm right, no one remembers; when I'm wrong, no one forgets". One suspects that there is a lot of forgetting done at 17 Battery Place, which since it was acquired early in Gleason's presidency has witnessed the challenges and achievements of two decades that outshine any similar span of time in the ILA's history.

DOROTHY HAYDEN

THE closest link that could be forged with the Irish Americans of New York is Dorothy Hayden, who for 41 years has been broadcasting every week and writing regularly about the music and culture of Ireland. Her "Irish Memories" programme on Station WEVD was taken over by her from her father, James A. Hayden, who began it in 1930 and had already pioneered Irish radio broadcasts on WGBS in the late 1920s.

Dorothy Hayden Cudahy—her husband John Cudahy is a leading tax consultant and has a degree in accountancy—made history in 1984 by being elected the first woman President of the Kilkenny Association and shattering an 80-year old tradition. She is also the first American-born person to hold the highest office in the association.

The Kilkenny Men's Social and Benevolent Association was established in 1904. In 1906 a Ladies Auxiliary was founded and in 1941 absorbed into the association under the new title Kilkenny Social and Benevolent Association with equality of membership. Dorothy Hayden is also a member of the officer board of the United Irish Counties' Association, of which the installing officer was Bill Burke, Senior Vice President of the Bank of Ireland.

James A. Hayden was born in Coole, Ballyragget, County Kilkenny. On Easter Sunday, 1916, in New York, he married Delia Brennan of Curry, County Sligo. Dorothy's love of Irish music, song and dance began when her father formed the "Irish Memories Entertainers", a group of which she became an important member. When James Hayden died in 1943 she took over the direction of this lively group which attained considerable recognition at Irish festivals, church concerts and dances.

The Irish dance hall boomed during the massive influxes of eimgration between 1920 and 1960 when many Irish and Irish American musicians, orchestras and band leaders rose to prominence. It was a time when the entire upper-west side of Manhatten was one huge Irish neighbourhood and the Irish Americans also occupied whole sections of Brooklyn, Staten Island and Queens. It was, especially, a time when the "Emerald Peninsula" of the Rockaways was a bastion of ethnic activity.

Dorothy Hayden talks of the beginning of the dance-hall era by recounting her father's arrival in America: "My father left home in Ballyragget on April 3rd, 1907, and sailed from Queenstown (now Cobh) on the *Majestic* of the White Star Line. They weathered eight days of hard sailing and a rash of seasickness. As my father wrote of the crossing in his journal: 'No one slept on the boat, not so much because of the rough seas, but because there was singing, dancing and music all night long'".

James Hayden waited a long time at Ellis Island before his cousin Ned Hayden came along in his police uniform after finishing duty at 4 p.m.. He recorded in his diary: "With bag and baggage we left Ellis Island for the Battery on April 14th and we walked to the Brooklyn Bridge which was then the terminal and took the Brooklyn trolley".

James Butler's grocery stores were generous in the giving of jobs to emigrants from Kilkenny. The Butlers were well-established, well-to-do owners of a chain of charge-account stores and young Hayden worked six days a week at the business. On the seventh, he stocked shelves and made up accounts. He also went to night school.

Tall, well-dressed and possessed of a mellifluous voice and impeccable diction, he was a natural for the early days of radio. He began on WGBS (the Gimbel Brothers' radio station) and soon became a celebrity on this new and exciting medium. As a result of his growing fame, he began to be asked to act as M.C. on the burgeoning ballroom circuit and for large parties throughout the city.

John B. Kelly, from Vermount, Menlough, County Galway, arrived in America in 1923 with a suitcase in one hand and his ten-button accordion in the other. James Hayden's journal records how the two met: "It was about the time that I entered radio that Alex Sunderson, a Swedish announcer at GBS, asked two Irish musicians who were working intermittently at the station to help him out, as he was not very good at calling out the Irish song titles. The two musicians were John 'Galway Accordion' Kelly and his partner, Michael Tully, a violinist who was John's neighbour back in Galway".

The meeting led to the formation of a group who were so successful that they began a live Saturday night radio show that was on the air for nearly two years. That programme was the forerunner of "Irish Memories", which Hayden began in 1930 and bequeathed to Dorothy who still broadcasts it every Sunday night at 11 o'clock to midnight.

Mickey Carton, a colleague and friend of Dorothy Hayden's, recalls how the young emigrant was greeted: "First an uncle or a cousin would go down to meet the young one just coming over and then there were four things you did for him right away. One, you got him a job. Two, you got him his first papers for eventual citizenship. Three, you got him a $1,000 insurance policy, and by his second or third night here you took him to one of the Irish dance halls. Usually you'd take him to the hall that 'belonged' to him, the Galway Hall, for instance, if he came from Galway. There he'd run into someone he met on the boat but lost at Ellis Island. Now they'd exchange addresses and more often than not remain friends for years thereafter. The dance halls were a part of the social transition".

Among the best-known halls in Manhattan were the Innisfail on 56th Street and Third Avenue; the Imperial Lyceum on 54th Street and Third Avenue; Donovan's Hall on Columbus Circle (where the Coliseum is now); the Banba Ballroom on 66th and Columbus Avenue, and Roger Sullivan's Columbus Avenue Ballroom on 104th Street. In upper Manhattan there was the Audubon Ballroom on 168th Street and Broadway.

There were 11 Irish dance halls in Harlem between 125th Street and 138th Street, including the Galway Hall, where John Kelly was a regular performer for 25 years. There too was the Melrah (Harlem spelt backwards) Social Club, a second-generation Irish organisation.

Elsewhere in the five boroughs, Brooklyn had its Erin's Isle and Pride of Erin Ballrooms; the Bronx had the Starlight (now a bus garage) and the Star of Munster on 138th Street and Willis Avenue.

On top of all these were the county halls—the Mayo Hall on 84th Street and Third Avenue; the Sligo House, the All-Ireland and the Tricolor Ballroom in the Bronx. The Leitrim and Clare halls were in Rockaway Beach. The concentration on counties from the West of Ireland is a reflection of both the poverty of that area and the tendency of people on the western seaboard to look to America rather than England.

Some of the principal halls in the 1950s, as the ballroom and emigration came to an end, were the Jaeger House on 85th Street and Lexington Avenue; Tuxedo Ballroom (a pointer here to growing affluence) on 59th Street and Madison Avenue, and Bill Fuller's City Center on 55th Street and Seventh Avenue.

"Most Irish men and women", says Dorothy Hayden, "were beautiful dancers and they loved the Irish waltzes in particular. For those who knew the more intricate traditional dances, the county halls were full of the sound of fiddles and concertinas. Matty Reardon's in Rockaway used to play those Kerry polkas and sets all night long".

In the heyday of the dance-hall age, James A. Hayden also became social editor of the *Irish Echo* for which he wrote a weekly column. On Saturday nights he would call at up to 16 dance halls, meet people and mention them in his column the following week. Mickey Carton recalls that it was a real big deal, a sign of social status, if you got your name mentioned.

"You'd cut it out and keep it in your wallet", he says, "and show it to a pretty girl you'd be trying to impress. It never failed!".

As safe social meeting places for young single Irish and Irish Americans the dance halls were invaluable. "A girl didn't have to worry", says Dorothy Hayden. "If she didn't meet a fella one night, so what! She would go with six or eight of her girlfriends and have a grand time anyway. We always felt protected. Somebody always knew us. We'd meet some friend of the family who would buy us Cokes, or the bartender might be somebody's uncle or cousin and he'd keep an eye on us. We'd think nothing of walking home by ourselves at a late hour. There was no fear of being mugged. But those were different times."

An acute observer of those palmy days, Charles T. Galbraith, wrote in 1981: "There was an air of innocence that seemed to surround the immigrants. The lyrics to many of the popular songs would be considered corny by today's standards and the jokes of the stand-up comics were clean. The humour of the day was simple and innocent, the partrons' laughs hearty and honest".

As Dorothy Hayden puts it: "It wasn't so much a matter of censorship. No one was interested in hearing the blue stuff. It just wasn't their style".

Big names abounded, the biggest of them Dennis McAuliffe and his I.R.A. Band. In the contemporary hall of fame were Dennis Day the singer; Sean O'Nolan the piper and poet; Jack Healy the musician and songwriter; Eddie Meehan the accordion player; the Flanagan Brothers on banjo and accordion, and a host of others including the Sligo fiddler Paddy Killoran.

The Innisfail was three ballrooms for the price of one—for Irish music only, for American music, and for both. The jitterbug craze was on but the Irish-only hall said: "No jitterbugging allowed".

After the war another boom began for the Irish ballroom and by the 1950s Dorothy Hayden, with Mickey Carton in her group, had become a household name in the Irish community. They appeared seven times on the Ed Sullivan Show between 1951 and 1957. During Easter Week, 1951, Dorothy Hayden and Mickey Carton played to standing-room-only crowds at the Palace Theatre, and in 1963 as a fitting crown to their careers they gave a special performance for President John F. Kennedy at the White House.

But it was the end of an era. Intermarriage, increasing affluence and mobility, and the ending of emigration from Ireland took their toll of the dance hall and other aspects of the ethnic consciousness. The music lives on and Dorothy Hayden plays Irish cabarets in the big East Coast cities. The renewed vitality of traditional music in Ireland has meant the appearance of many Irish groups such as the Chieftains and De Danaan on American tours, and many second and third generation Irish Americans are rediscovering their heritage through the music.

Dorothy's Hayden's is now only one of many Irish radio programmes flourishing in New York City being broadcast over Fordham's WFUV, Eugene V. Debs's WEVD; WHBI and WVOX among others. Her programme is broadcast from the Empire State Building and reaches Connecticut, New York State and New Jersey under the sponsorship of Allied Irish Banks, among others.

Among the thousands of people Dorothy Hayden has interviewed are Paddy Moloney of the Chieftains, the late Paddy O'Keeffe of the G.A.A.; Con Murphy and all the other Presidents of the G.A.A.; Bernadette McAliskey; Peter Barry, John Wilson, Frank Cluskey, Síle de Valera and Governor Hugh Carey.

Dorothy and her husband John Cudahy, whose parents came from Inagh in County Clare, have one son, Seán, who is 35 and an ex-President of the County Clare Association. Seán works for the U.S. Government and was recently elected a director of the St. Patrick's Day Parade Committee under Judge James J. Comerford, a native of Coolraheen, Castlecomer, County Kilkenny, and second vice president of Dorothy Hayden Cudahy's Kilkenny Association officer board. The installing officer of the Association was John Thornton, editor of the *Irish Echo*.

Dorothy and John first went to Ireland together in 1957 and they have made the journey 12 times since. When she is away, she tapes her Sunday night programme in advance. They have also gone to Hawaii and New Zealand with the Emerald Golfers, of which Mick Morrissey is President ("A lot of footballers and hurlers are now playing golf", she says). They went to Australia too and were impressed not only by the Sydney Opera House but by the guide who showed them around. She was a Vandeleur from Clare whose people laid out the streets of Kilrush.

In November, 1981, Dorothy Hayden Cudahy, had another

memorable experience. Tomás Cardinal Ó Fiaich said Mass in St. Patrick's Cathedral, New York, with the late Terence Cardinal Cooke. The Irish Consul-General at the time was Seán Ó hUiginn, now Ambassador to Saudi Arabia. He read one of the lessons: the other was read by Dorothy Hayden.

Mickey sums up what Dorothy Hayden and the Irish identity are about:

"When my daughter was younger, her bedroom was full of the Beatles. To her, my music and all Irish music was square. Now that she's older, she's taken a whole new view, and all on her own. I've noticed that she has bought some Irish song books and is learning all the words to many of the traditional songs. I've also noticed that she's wearing her Celtic cross and Claddagh ring lately, even to social affairs. It seems to her that it's nice to be Irish. Thanks be to God, and our children, our heritage will live on".

EDWARD L. HENNESSY, Jr.

IN 1983, one of the largest and smoothest corporate mergers in U.S. history took place when Allied Corporation joined forces with the Bendix Corporation. The principal architect of this design was Edward L. Hennessy, Jr., Chairman of the Board and Chief Executive Officer of Allied, which he had joined only four years previously.

Edward Hennessy had come a long way from an Irish neighbourhood in Boston to command the 29th-largest company in the United States with sales last year of $10 billion. Although the received wisdom has it that it was the election of John F. Kennedy to the Presidency of the United States that removed the last remaining barrier to ultimate acceptance of the Irish American, his fellow Bostonian believes firmly that "Kennedy was *not* responsible. Education is the key. My father was the first of our family to go to high school, and a generation later I went to college".

Allied Corporation, based in Morris Township, New Jersey, was incorporated in New York in 1920 as Allied Chemical Corporation and changed its title in 1981. Lehrman Commercial Paper Inc. describes Allied as "a diversified multinational company" with, before the merger, interests in chemicals, fibres and plastics, oil and gas, electrical and electronic products, and health and scientific products. Then in early 1983 the company acquired Bendix Corporation, "a diversified manufacturer of aerospace, electronic products and systems, automotive products and industrial equipment" with a net income of $138 millon on revenues of $4.1 billion in the year to September, 1982. The transaction was valued at about $1.8 billion.

Hennessy says: "Putting two large companies together effectively is one of the business world's greatest challenges. Conceiving and negotiating a strategically sound acquisition is usually easier than making the merger work. This consolidation, I'm pleased to say, is working very well. The big Bendix automative and aerospace businesses are still being run by the managers who ran them before and most of the key Bendix executives have chosen to stay and become part of Allied's corporate staff. The Bendix merger is already doing for Allied what we expected it would do—it has increased domestic income, reduced our dependence on oil and gas, diversified our operations into higher-tech, higher value-added products, and made Allied much less capital-intensive.

"When we negotiated the merger we publicly committed ourselves to cutting $1 billion off the $2.6 billion debt of the combined companies by the end of 1984. In fact we achieved this target by November 1983.

"Because of our financial strength we were also able to acquire two other, much smaller, companies in 1983—Semi-Alloys who make components used in manufacturing computer chips, and Instrumentation Laboratory who make sophisticated instruments used in medical diagnosis and industrial analysis. We will make more acquisitions as we see growth opportunities.

"In 1978, Allied's total spending on research and development was $56 million. In 1983, with Bendix, we spent $394 million on R and D and carried out another $173 million worth of research funded by customers, mainly in government. That's a change in five years".

Hennessy's reference to reducing Allied's dependence on oil and gas is to the proportion of the company's income generated by hydrocarbons, which the merger has reduced from 77 per cent in 1982 to 43 per cent in 1983. Somewhat dented by media speculation which emphasised the difficulty that Allied would have in handling the large merger-related debt, investor confidence was restored. There was a 70 per cent-plus increase in the value of Allied's common stock between the end of 1982 and the end of 1983, compared with a 20 per cent increase in the Dow Jones Industrial average in the same period.

A company spokesman quotes Ovid's *Heroides* as evidence of Edward Hennessy's prescience: "If you would marry wisely, marry your equal". (Ovid himself married twice in early life at the desire of his parents and divorced each wife in turn. He later married again a woman whom he seems to have loved sincerely).

Allied's foreign operations accounted for 24.4 per cent of sales and 66.7 per cent of income from operations last year. With a worldwide workforce of nearly 118,000, the company has 70 plants in the chemical division operating in the U.S. and Canada. Net daily production from Union Texas Petroleum, Allied's oil and gas subsidiary, in its world operations was 86,000 barrels of crude oil and condensate, and 297 million cubic feet of natural gas. Reserves were thought to be 495 million barrels of oil equivalent by the year's end and drilling resulted in a 20 per cent success ratio on exploratory and 95 per cent on development wells. Indonesia, the North Sea and Pakistan are among the many areas on which $623 million is being spent in 1984.

In the Automotive Sector, Allied last year operated 39 plants in the U.S. and another 52 in South America, Australia and Western Europe with a heavy concentration on France (16) and Spain (10). The primarily Bendix Aerospace-Electronics Group has 23 plants in the U.S. and Canada and derives almost 80 per cent of its revenues from government-related markets—all of which are projected to grow in 1984.

The new Industrial and Technology Sector was set up last year to gather together under one umbrella a group of businesses that had come into Allied's hands through acquisition. If it were to be given a school report, the teacher's remark might be: "Showing signs of improvement: could do better". Some 43 plants are in the U.S. and 19 in Canada, South America, Puerto Rico and Western Europe.

Edward Hennessy was recruited from United Technologies Corporation in 1979. In May, he was President and Chief Executive Officer and by December he had become Chairman and Chief Executive Officer. At United Technologies, which he joined in 1972 as Senior Vice President, Finance and Administration, he had been from 1977 Executive Vice President, Group Vice President Systems and Equipment Group and Chief Financial Officer.

At Allied, one of the proudest boasts is the quality of the medical service provided. Each plant has a facility for X-rays and blood-tests, and the programme on alcoholism involves having a counsellor in all the factories. Ed Hennessy claims they have a 70 per cent recovery rate for alcoholics. "I firmly believe in the efficacy of Alcoholics Anonymous", he says, "with its emphasis on taking life a day at a time. I am convinced that anybody attending AA meetings for two years has a very good chance of recovery".

Tall, tanned and very much in control of himself, Hennessy takes a piece of paper off the table and reads: "Says here that my great grandfather came to America from Ireland at the age of nine".

Grehan in her *Irish Family Names* says that there were at least four Hennessy septs spread out over Leinster and Munster and there is a number of places called Ballyhennessy in Counties Clare, Cork and Kerry. They had their original stronghold in North Offaly and another branch of this purely Gaelic family lived west of Dublin on the north bank of the River Liffey. "After the Norman invasion", she says, "they were dispersed and they spread south to Cork, Limerick and Tipperary..."

The most famous internationally were the Hennessys who entered the service of France after the Treaty of Limerick in 1691. Richard

Hennessy, wounded in the Battle of Fontenoy, settled in Cognac and in 1765 established the company that has made Hennessy brandy world renowned. Today in France the Hennessy line remains unbroken and the names Maurice, Patrick and Kilian are still to be found on the board of directors.

Edward Hennessy has hired two firms to research on his roots, which go back to 1800. In May, 1983, he made a journey to Mitchelstown, County Cork, to see the graveyard in which a daughter of his great great grandfather was buried in 1870 at the age of 29. She lies in the Catholic cemetery. It was by no means his first visit to Ireland and is most unlikely to be his last because his pride of ancestry is a real force in his life.

His great grandfather William arrived in America in 1842 and was a drummer in the Battle of Bull Run in 1861, the first year of the Civil War. Bull Run is in Virginia and the battle was an overwhelming victory for the Confederate Army of the South. Among the Confederate commanders was Colonel Thomas J. Jackson of whom Brigadier-General B.E. Bee said: "Look, there is Jackson standing like a stone wall". The name Stonewall Jackson stuck.

William Hennessy's son Edward Joseph settled in Boston in 1871, when the Irish, says Edward Hennessy, "were in the city in droves. They could clean shoes, be policemen, firemen, garbage collectors or porters. With a little education, they could become teachers. But none of them ran a business because Boston was a WASP communitys, and you were not expected to come out of your ethnic pocket".

Edward Joseph worked on the elevated railway and lied about his age, saying that he was 60 until he died at over 80. His son, Edward L. Hennessy's father, is alive and well and living in Boston at the age of 84. His wife, the former Celena Doucette, was a French Canadian from Quebec province and died in 1981. Ed Hennessy's only brother lives in Maine and was formerly a naval officer. (He himself was in the Naval Reserve for many years).

He was born in March, 1928, in West Roxbury, Boston, and went to public school there. After high school he spent three years as a seminarian in the University of Notre Dame in Indiana. He then graduated in business studies in 1955 from Fairleigh Dickinson University, Rutherford, New Jersey, where he is now Chairman of the Board. He went on to attend the Law School of New York University, but all this academic achievement was nocturnal. By day he worked for Textron from 1951 to 1956 and for Lair Seigler up to 1960.

His first senior job was as Controller of the International Electronic Corporation, a subsidiary of I.T.T. in New York. In 1962 he was appointed Controller of I.T.T. Europe, living in England and Belgium, and then the pace quickens. ("I always say I couldn't hold a job. After all, my father worked for the same company for over 50 years.") Heublein, Inc., was the next move, and there he was Vice President, Finance, from 1965 to 1968, rising to Senior Vice President, Administration and Finance, from 1969 to 1972. Then came United Technologies and the wheel is come full circle.

Such a career in such companies provides a strong argument if not for the round man, at least for the administrator as against the technocrat. And this contention gains added weight from looking at some of Edward Hennessy's memberships and organisations: the John F. Kennedy Center for the Performing Arts; the Tri-County Scholarship Fund (N.J.) of which he is a founder with the Bishop of Paterson ("I make a lot of speeches around here raising funds for scholarships for third-generation blacks to get them out of the ghetto"); the Catholic University of America in Washington, D.C., and Lafayette College, Pennsylvania, of both of which he is a trustee.

Like Gene Sullivan of Borden, he was a member of the President's Private Sector Survey on Cost Control. He is a member of the Conference Board, Inc., and again like Sullivan, of the Economic Club of New York. And he is not a member of the Ireland Fund? "I've never been asked to join".

Married to the former Ruth Schilling of New Jersey, he has two adopted children, one of whom, Elizabeth Ruth, was born in Ireland 26 years ago and is at Manchester Community College. Their son, Michael Edward, is 28, and works for Pratt and Whitney in Hartford, Connecticut. The Hennessys lived in Hartford, Connecticut, for 17 years and have had roots in Hartford for 20 years.

"I was taught by my mother to be competitive", he says "She was a women before her time, playing professional hockey in Boston in the early 1900s. I've always been like that, disliking the idea of welfare and staying home. I had to get out to work to survive. My father never left Boston. Both my brother and I did.

"Among the people I admire are Harold Geneen who was head of I.T.T., and Cardinal Cushing who rose out of South Boston to become the first Cardinal Archbishop who hadn't come from the North American College in Rome. I'd like to meet Cardinal Ó Fiaich some time".

DENIS P. KELLEHER

"IT is not completely absurd to assert that as long as some people continue to think of themselves as Americans and simultaneously as Irishmen and Kerrymen, the United States will be saved from the worst prospects of the modern world". That was written by Senator Daniel Patrick Moynihan in an essay on "Preserving Irish-American Identity" which he contributed to a book called *Kerrymen* published in 1981 to celebrate the centenary of the Kerrymen's Patriotic and Benevolent Association of New York.

Senator Moynihan is himself of Kerry extraction. His people came from Headford Junction and his very name means "man from Munster". In 1963 he and Nathan Glazer published *Beyond the Melting Pot*, a study of New York's Italians, Jews, Puerto Ricans, Blacks and Irish. Their conclusion, tentative though it was, seemed shocking at the time: "The notion that the intense and unprecedented mixture of ethnic and religious groups in American life was soon to blend into a homogeneous end product has outlived its usefulness and also its credibility".

Denis P. Kelleher, Chief Executive Officer of the Wall Street Clearing Company, was the editor of *Kerrymen* and has inscribed a copy of that fine publication to this writer thus: "When you visit Kerry, I am sure both will be enriched". Like the other Irish-born dreamers of the American dream in this book, he remembers vividly his arrival in America. "I landed on January 26th, 1958, which was a Sunday. Next day I joined Merrill Lynch, Pierce, Fenner and Smith as a runner". He spent the next seven years climbing up the ladder at Merrill Lynch and going to night school at St. John's University, where he majored in accountancy.

So well did Denis Kelleher get on that Merrill Lynch offered him the job of managing their Chicago office, an offer he declined because he had just got married and wanted to stay in New York. He had also by then completed a six-month programme with the U.S. Army at Fort Knox, Kentucky, and he was on the reserve for 5½ years.

From 1966 for three years Kelleher became Assistant to the managing partner at Neuberger and Berman. Then he was associated with Ruane Cunniff where as Vice President he developed and operated a clearing function. As he puts it, he was "in the money management business on a discretionary basis", achieving the best record on Wall Street and acting also as Vice President of Ruane Cunniff's Sequoia Fund which was in the top 10 performing mutual funds for 15 years.

The top beckoned and he became President of Ruane Cunniff in 1975, working with colleagues, "a nice group of people", who all had Harvard Business School backgrounds. In the same year, which saw the disappearance of fixed commissions, he founded and became President of the Discount Brokerage Corporation of America which was recently sold to Norstar Bank for close to $40 million. Discount Brokerage also has a wholly-owned subsidiary, Tweedy Browne Clearing Corporation, in which he is involved. All these firms are members of the New York Stock Exchange.

Then came 1981 and the formation of the Wall Street Clearing Company with Denis Kelleher as Chief Executive Officer. This was a joint venture with Kansas City Southern Industries Inc., which is primarily a railroad holding company that wanted a larger presence in the financial services area. ("This", says Denis Kelleher wryly, "is the buzz-word, financial services"). "They asked me to go 50-50 with them to get that presence. What we do is buying, selling, trading in securities for 50 other broker/dealers, 900 banks, four mutual funds and five insurance companies. We process over $20 billion worth a year and by the next three years we expect that to be $100 billion. We work on all major stock exchanges and over-the-counter markets and process margin, cash and option accounts".

From Kansas City Southern Industries' point of view, they work with Wall Street Clearing through their financial record-keeping company DST Systems and find that WSCC has given DST direct exposure to the processing requirements of brokerage accounting and provided access to brokerage services for DST clients and their customers.

Kansas City's core business is Kansas City Southern Lines, which has 1,663 miles of railway, "serving the world from the heartland of America" as they like to put it. That heartland consists of the six states of Missouri, Kansas, Arkansas, Oklahoma, Texas and Louisiana, and the company has a motor truck subsidiary with authority to operate in five adjoining states. One of the railway's prime concerns is the carriage of coal, and it claims its capacity in that area "far exceeds even the most optimistic figures presented by developers of the proposed coal slurry pipeline". The system, which has 320 locomotives and over 70,000 goods wagons, is an all-freight concern with Deramus Yard in Shreveport, Louisiana, as its main centre of operations.

Railway marshalling yards in Middle America seem a far cry from 17 Battery Place in Manhattan, but Denis Kelleher's tentacles stretch much farther than New York. He has a company called National Realty Services in Pennsylvania Avenue, Washington, D.C., established in 1983 as a real estate tax syndication company which buys properties, forms partnerships, and sells units of $50,000 to investors who get income-tax write-off benefits. These units are available only to investors whose net worth is $1 million.

National Realty employs about 50 people; Discount Brokerage a couple of hundred, and Wall Street Clearing as many again. Another of Denis Kelleher's enterprises is a joint venture with another brokerage firm. Formed early in 1984, Somerset Capital Management manages corporate pension money.

He is also a director of Libra Funds, an exciting development consisting of two new mutual funds designed to meet the needs of today's independent woman investor. They are managed by Somerset Capital and are the result of sophisticated research indicating that there is a substantial market for new financial products for women investors concerned with financial independence and interested in a prudent, consistent investment programme.

The women interviewed for the study were "impatient with financial jargon, interested in the concepts behind the terminology and wanted access to clear, detailed information".

Four of the nine directors of Libra Funds are women. Elizabeth McCormack is former President of Manhattanville College and philanthropic adviser to the Rockefeller family; Letitia Baldridge is a writer and was chief of staff for Mrs. John F. Kennedy; Wendy Rue is President and founder of the National Association for Female Executives, and Amelia Jones, formerly of Hallac Associates, the New York investment advisers, is director of investor services for the Libra Funds.

How is it all done? By working from 7.30 a.m. to 8 o'clock at night and carrying the briefcase home at weekends. "I'm hoping to cut down", says this 44-year-old Kerryman who finds that "people here still consider I have a brogue. TH sounds are still hard to pronounce for me". Among his memberships is the Whitehall Club, mainly peopled by shippers. There he gives a monthly lunch for 20 out-of-town brokers.

"We're in a high-tension business", he say, and goes on to praise his fellow Irishman Tony O'Reilly, whom he regards as one of the top 10 executives in the United States. This admiration he shares with many others including Brother John Driscoll, President of Iona College in New Rochelle, who feels that "O'Reilly knows where Irish power lies in the U.S., second only to the Jews in economic influence and affluence".

Denis Kelleher was born in Gneeveguilla, Rathmore, in County Kerry, where his father was a shoemaker. He went to the local National School and then to St. Brendan's College, Killarney. He is one of a family of four. His sister is married to Gerry Wilson from County Leitrim and living on Long Island. His brother Bertie is vice-principal of Turner's Cross College in Cork City, and his brother John works on the Adult Education Programme for Cork-Kerry and is editor of the *Sliabh Luachra* magazine, which is devoted to the traditional music "so integral", as Denis Kelleher says, "to that part of the country".

His wife is the former Carol Cieslewicz from Brooklyn, an Irish American, and they have three children. Denis, who in 17; Seán (16), and Colleen (15), are all at high school on Staten Island, where the Kellehers have lived on Emerson Hill for 15 years, "It's a unique place to live", Denis Kelleher says, "because it is preserved. There are no street lights and no sidewalks. Private patrols keep it secure, and it is only a ferry ride from there to work". He is Chairman of the local development committee and Vice Chairman of Snug Harbor Cultural Center.

Music is endemic. His favourite is the Kerry set danced to the accompaniment of a fiddle and a melodeon. Colleen plays the piano and the children have all spent some time in Ireland. Denis Junior and Seán have spent a whole summer on the bog and kept a daily diary which they presented to the proud father when they came home. "It's important that they remember their heritage", he feels.

"I'm not a joiner", says Denis Kelleher. "I have a warm spot for Ireland and I'm a member of the Kerrymen's Association, but I don't want a high profile on the Irish American scene. The Friendly Sons of St. Patrick have a black-tie dinner for St. Patrick's Day and it would make you proud to be Irish that night to see all the distinguished Irish Americans gathered there".

The strength of Kerry in New York is reflected in a photograph in *Kerrymen* of the editorial staff and centennial committee. There one sees Professor John P. McCarthy of Fordham University, the son of

Iveragh immigrants and author of an essay on Michael J. Quill and the Transport Workers' Union; Nick Murphy from Tarbert, who is Manager—U.S.Treasury Operations of the International Telephone and Telegraph Corporation and a columnist in the *Irish Echo*; Joe Murphy, John O'Connor, Michael Kennedy, Tigue Murphy, Tim Murphy, Denis P. Kelleher in his capacity as editor of this book; Maurice J. Bric and Daniel Daly.

Maurice Bric was born in Cahirciveen, is a graduate of University College Cork, and the Johns Hopkins University, and is Andrew W. Mellon Fellow at the University of Pennyslvania. He contributed an essay on "The Rightboy Protest in County Kerry". Timothy J. Murphy, Tigue Murphy and John O'Connor are past presidents of the Kerrymen's Association of New York.

Daniel Daly, of Kerry stock, is a native of Long Island. He holds a doctorate in English from St. John's University and is a teacher and poet. In *Kerrymen* he publishes a tender and moving portrait of "Corridan S.J.", the Rev. John M. Corridan, a Jesuit who led the post-war insurrection against the stranglehold of the International Longshoremen's Association . . . . . "a tall man in a world of diminutive card carriers", and a man, of course, of Kerry blood.

Missing from the photograph is one of the editors, Brother Charles B. Quinn, Professor of English and Special Assistant to President John G. Driscoll of Iona College, New Rochelle. Brother Quinn, who once taught in the Christian Brothers' School in Synge Street, Dublin, contributes to *Kerrymen* "A Glance at the Past", a scholarly examination of the records of the Kerrymen's Association donated in 1979 to Iona College.

Among the many other distinguished contributors whom Denis Kelleher so sedulously collected to form this book was William D. Griffin, Professor of History at St. John's University, Queens, New York. A son of Kerry immigrants, he is also Archivist of the American Irish Historical Society in New York. In *Kerrymen* he has a fascinating essay on "Kerrymen in the French Revolution", but his great contribution to Irish American studies is his book "A Portrait of the Irish in America", published in the same year as *Kerrymen* (1981), lavishly illustrated from a bewildering variety of sources, and with an introduction by Senator Daniel Patrick Moynihan, who began this chapter for us and provides a fitting end to it:

"One can mourn for a virtual ghost town like Tuosist, which saw its

1841 population of 7,485 fall to 899 in 1966. But one must also read of Kerry's successes—Daniel O'Connell and St. Brendan among them, as well as thousands of Kerrymen who came to the shores of America to claim a fortune quite unimaginable to those left behind". That surely says what Denis Kelleher is about.

Dorothy Ann Kelly

IT was no accident that the struggle to free women began in America after the Revolution and developed muscles along with the movement to free the slaves. During the Revolution Judith Sargent Murray said that woman needed knowledge to envisage new goals and grow by reaching for them. That was a decade before Mary Wollstonecraft began the feminist movement in England.

Thomas Paine, whose seminal influence on Paul O'Dwyer is pin-pointed elsewhere in this book, was in 1775 among the first to condemn the position of women "even in countries where they may be esteemed the most happy, constrained in their desires in the disposal of their goods, robbed of freedom and will by the laws, the slaves of opinion. . . ."

The first Woman's Rights Convention was held in Seneca Falls, New York, in 1848, and summed up the grievances of woman against man in specific detail. "He has denied her the facilities for obtaining a thorough education, all college being closed against her", ran one charge, notwithstanding the fact that eleven years earlier Mount Holyoke had been established to give women their first opportunity of an education equal to men's.

In 1904 the order of Ursuline nuns opened the College of New Rochelle, New York, in response to the specific needs of young Irish Catholic women. The college now has as President a very distinguished educator, Sister Dorothy Ann Kelly, who sees the recent outward movement of the college as being some kind of recompense to the people of New York City for the support they lent to New Rochelle in its formative years.

Betty Friedan in her thoroughly documented work of 20 years ago, *The Feminine Mystique*, says: "A recent study of 50 women college graduates in an eastern suburb and city, the year after the oldest child had left home, showed that, with very few exceptions, the only women who had any interests to pursue—in work, in community activities, or in the arts—had acquired them in college. The ones who lacked such interests were not acquiring them now; they slept late, in their 'empty nests', and looked forward only to death".

In 1969 Sister Kelly was Dean of the College when it became co-educational. The School of Arts and Sciences, however, remained single-sex and in that sense the college remains one of the 115 women's colleges left in the United States. The Rev. Mother M.R. Falls was President in that watershed year and she had a student enrolment of 940 with 88 teachers.

Now the School of Arts and Sciences alone has 725 students; the Graduate School has 950; the School of New Resources, which began in 1972 as part of a national movement for adult students, has 3,000; there are 600 in the co-educational Baccalaureate Program for returning adults; 400 in a co-educational course which was requested by the Municipal Workers' Union and has its headquarters and five locations in New York City; and there are 300 in the School of Nursing.

On the theme of women's colleges, Sister Dorothy Ann waxes eloquent: "There are still advantages for some women in coming into an atmosphere that is non-competitive with men. For example, the whole athletic scene is transformed when women can ignore the relative physical strengths of the sexes. There may come a day when the opportunities for men and women are really equal and then we'll have to look again. But in the meantime there are decided advantages to having full attention given to young women's needs and enabling them to hold all the offices that student life offers.

"There's also the question of role models. Take a simple thing like putting on a dramatic production. Obviously there are male and female parts in a play, but in a co-ed college the men would do the building of the sets and the hauling of the props while the women would sew the costumes and do the make-up. You can see the benefits to women's self-confidence and development in taking on all these tasks for themselves".

This line of argument is taken up by Sister Dorothy Ann Kelly's co-Ursuline and personal friend, Sister Jean-Baptiste Nicholson, Principal of the Ursuline Academy, New Rochelle, a Catholic girls' school for ages seven to 18.

Sister Jean-Baptiste says: "Separation is a great advantage at this age" (she is referring to girls over 12). "Girls are not anxious to be academically smarter than boys in a co-ed school because then they won't be dated. Positions of leadership are open here whereas if this school were co-ed the girls would let the boys take them. At this age, the boy benefits more than the girl in a co-ed situation because of the stimulation he feels to be smarter and the refining influence the girls have on him.

"One of the reasons why women are sometimes not in the forefront is the cost to their femininity. The ideal surely is for men and women to be separate but equal. The real world is OK if women have come to believe in their own abilities. Token women in business are all we have now. But women are moving. They have to move. Those who are now in their 20s and early 30s will make the major impact".

Sister Jean-Baptiste sits on the Board of Trustees of the College of New Rochelle. "Dorothy Ann is so unusual", she says. "She's a leader in the independent colleges. Not just the Catholic ones; not just the women's ones—she's a leader, and a good friend".

The Ursuline order was founded in 1535, so its 450th anniversary is in 1985. Its founder was Angela Merici da Brescia, who died in 1540. Four years later its institution was confirmed by Pope Paul III and at this time the order received its present name from its patron, St. Ursula of Cologne. In 1572 Gregory XIII placed it officially under the Augustinian rule. Education is its principal work and it spread from Brescia, Italy, to France; then to Ireland and the United States. Now it has houses in every continent.

Sister Dorothy Ann Kelly was born in the Bronx. Her father's people were Kellys and Geraghtys who came to New York in 1840, and her mother, who died when she was a child, was a McCauley whose forebears were Belfast. She has visited Northern Ireland and met the Peace Women, Mairéad Corrigan and Betty Williams, whose work she admired enormously. In 1982 she visited the South.

As a commuter student, she attended the College of New Rochelle, where she majored in history in 1951. She began to teach at New Rochelle in 1957, and did her master's degree in Church history at the Catholic University of America in Washington, D.C. At Notre Dame in Indiana she did her doctorate in American intellectual history. She became President of the college in 1972 and has transformed the philosophy of the college by initiating the School of New Resources, the Baccalaureate Program for returning adults and the co-operative enterprise she devised with the Municipal Workers' Union.

Bringing the college to the inner city is an unusual concept when the college is 40 or 50 miles away. As Betty Friedan has said: "For women as well as men, education is and must be the matrix of human evolution. If today American women are finally breaking out of the housewife trap in search of new identity, it is quite simply because so many women have had a taste of higher education—unfinished, unfocused, but still powerful enough to force them on".

A woman graduate of Swarthmore College, Pennsylvania, says that she worried a lot at first about having dates and getting married. Then she got interested in what she was doing and stopped worrying:

"It's as if you've made some kind of shift. You begin to feel your competence in doing things. Like a baby learning to walk. Your mind begins to expand. You find your own field. And that's a wonderful thing. The love of doing the work and the feeling there's something there and you can trust it. It's worth the unhappiness. They say a man has to suffer to grow; maybe something like that has to happen to women too. You begin not to be afraid to be yourself".

Mary Wollstonecraft, the English pioneer of women's rights, and an Irishwoman by descent, earned her living by teaching between 1778 and 1788. Then she worked for Johnson the publisher as reader and translator, and while she was in this job she met Tom Paine and like him wrote an *Answer to Burke's Reflections on the French Revolution*. She wrote a great number of books including *Vindication of the Rights of Women* (1792) and in 1797 she married the famous English writer William Godwin, a dissenting minister whose faith was shaken by the study of the French philosophers. Mary died in child-birth and the poet Shelley married their daughter Mary in 1816.

In the environment of New Rochelle where Tom Paine once lived and where his cottage is still preserved, it is perhaps not impertinent to draw to a close the story of Dorothy Ann Kelly, educator extraordinary, with a quotation from Mary Wollstonecraft's *Vindication*:

"For my arguments, Sir, are debated by a disinterested Spirit—I plead for my sex, not for myself. Independence I have long considered the grand blessing of life, the basis of every virtue—and independence I will ever secure by contracting my wants, though I were to live on a barren heath".

JOHN E. LAWE

WHEN John Lawe was growing up in Kilglass, Strokestown, Co. Roscommon, he was one of 10 children on a 60-acre farm. He followed a set social pattern by leaving school in Slatta, Kilglass, at the age of 13 to earn money on the county council road works. He rose to the position of ganger or foreman there until he got a job on Kilbarry bog as a "grade A ganger" with Bord na Móna, the peat development authority. That was in 1945 and his wages were £6.18s. a week (about $33 at the then prevailing rate of exchange). He had charge of 100 men for that money.

When his cousin, Tom Cawley, came home from America on vacation, he so impressed young Lawe with his fine clothes that Lawe found the courage to ask him: "How do you get to America?" With money he had saved in the Post Office, he bought his ticket for America, and after a farewell party in the Tower Ballroom in Tarmonbarry he was soon on board the liner *Aquitania* bound for New York. Because of a strike in New York port the ship was diverted to Halifax, Nova Scotia, and he finally reached New York in time for the St. Patrick's Day Parade of 1949. Canada was covered in snow that March and on the journey he saw for the first time horses pulling sleds.

Work did not come easily, but after three weeks he got a job at $37 in a hotel working a six-day shift. The first sign of his ultimate career came a year later when a friend got him a job as a cleaner with the Fifth Avenue Coach Company.

Following the time-honoured Irish tradition, John Lawe soon became active in his union, the Transport Workers, as a maintenance shop steward at the 132nd Street Garage (known as "the barn"); a picket captain in the 29-day strike of 1953, a transportation section chairman in 1955, and then head of all sections of the Fifth Avenue Line.

In 1953, he had switched jobs to become a bus driver and operated a bus until 1968 when he became vice-president of Local 100 of the Transport Workers Union and a full-time official. "I've never looked back since", he says. The Manhattan and Bronx Surface Transit Operating Authority (MABSTOA) was created in 1962 and Lawe became the union's division 1 recording secretary. Two years later he was elected division chairman and played an active role in the 12-day New York City bus and subway strike in 1966.

It was when he became a permanent T.W.U. official that John Lawe's skill in negotiation began to blossom, and since 1971 he has led contract negotiations for his members on private bus lines in Westchester and on the private Manhattan and Queens lines that make up the Queens division which he helped to establish.

Lawe found himself thrust into a tough situation in April, 1980, when T.W.U. Local 100—of which he had become president in 1977—became the first public employee union to negotiate its contract that year. As a result he found that the attention of business, labour, the media and the public was focussed on his every decision as the members opted for strike action.

Trying to steer a highly volatile and disaffected membership suffering from financial setbacks in previous years, he handled his role as president and negotiator with a fine balance of toughness and sagacity which ultimately won a four-to-one vote for his decision to order his men and women back to work after his executive deadlocked 22-22 on the recommendations of a fact-finding group.

The 1980 strike was front page news every day with headlines such as "$1 million in fines levied on 2 unions in transit strike: Lawe still defiant: Won't order T.W.U. back". It was only the second city-wide transport strike in New York's history and in the result a fair contract was won, though at the cost of fines and loss of pay. "In the T.W.U", says Lawe, "we have always known that something worth fighting for often carries a high price tag".

The Transport Workers' Union of America in April, 1984, marked its golden jubilee. The triumphs of 50 years, and some of the defeats, were marked in the rhetoric, but the spotlight which was turned on Michael J. Quill as the putative founder of the Union did not play around the Communist edges.

Mike Quill was born in Kilgarvan, County Kerry, and with two of his brothers was one of the hard-line republicans who left Ireland in the great immigration wave of the 1920s. Al Smith was Governor of New York, Jimmy Walker was Mayor, the West Side from the 40s up to Harlem was an Irish neighbourhood and there was little attempt at enforcing prohibition. It was a good time to be Irish.

Quill worked with the private Interborough Rapid Transit Company and spoke frequently of the need for the subway workers to break the company union. But it was only when John Santo, the Communist organiser, recruited Mike Quill and others to form the Transport Workers' Union that progress began to be made in the fight against harsh conditions.

Unemployment stood at 12 million in a labour force that was only half the size it is today, and management had imposed a 10% pay cut on transport workers on top of the abolition of the workers' pension plan. If pay was bad, conditions were worse. Drivers and conductors often had to report at 5 a.m. and remain on hand until 9 p.m. to get an "ordinary", that is 12-hour, day's work. There were no days off and any man who took one on his own faced the loss of one to three days' work as a penalty.

The T.W.U. was born in a cafeteria on Columbus Circle on April 12th, 1934, with the Communist Party, as Professor John P. McCarthy of Fordham University has admirably recorded, providing the publicity, administration and organisational knowledge for the enthusiastic and willing Irishmen. By November, Quill had become President of the Union and a full-time organiser paid by the Communist Party.

As part of the price for its support, the Communist Party demanded Quill's rigid adherence to the party line, even to accepting the Soviet-German pact of August, 1939, which upset most left-wing people in America. Mayor La Guardia and ultimately the national leader of the Congress of Industrial Organisations, John L. Lewis, broke with Quill and there was dissent in his own union's ranks, especially when the House Un-American Activities Committee in the spring of 1940 began to investigate Communism in the Union. Quill was enjoying himself.

In furtherance of the revolution, the Communist Party planned that the T.W.U. should make unreasonable demands against management and an 11-day strike was carried out against a major private bus-line which was willing to negotiate. A small pay rise was won but the next strike against the subway authority was aborted by the German invasion of the Soviet Union. Quill became enthusiastic about the war and continued to avoid any more strikes.

Was Mike Quill a Communist? He never admitted that he was and while he handomely repaid the debt he owed the Party, Professor McCarthy says: "Quill's was not the temperament or nature to take an ideology or *Weltanschauung* like Marxism too seriously. After all, he was a Kerry peasant moved by immediate concerns such as getting a union organised, keeping it in existence, and maintaining the support of the membership. Consequently, when the time was ripe Quill could be expected to dump the Red secretariat whose primary loyalties went beyond the Union to the revolution". And when he did begin to purge the Communists in 1948, he did so with all the skill of the demagogue that he had learned at their hands.

In the meantime the Transport Union had made giant strides. By Christmas of 1937, the Union had contracts covering 33,000 New York transport workers. Two months earlier John L. Lewis told 22,000 workers at the T.W.U.'s first convention in Madison Square Garden: "I know of no parallel accomplishment on the part of a newly-formed union".

Around the United States the Union spread, and in 1942 it moved into the airline industry. Now it also controls gas workers, railway men, space workers and some federal and local government employee groups under its International President, William G. Lindner.

But it all began in New York with what became Local 100, now headed up by John Lawe who presides over the destinies of the city's 36,000 transport workers. "It was our local here in New York", he says, "that produced our first two international presidents. Mike Quill, our founder, guided the T.W.U. with dedication and guts until his death shortly after the 1966 New York transit strike. Matthew Guinan then took over and served with the same distinction until his retirement in 1979.

"At special times like our 50th anniversary, our history should be reflected upon and remembered fondly. Anyone who believes that we in Local 100 would be enjoying what we enjoy today—which is the best transit contract in the country—without the blood, sweat and tears shed by our founders is either naive or terribly misinformed". And Lawe recalls the *Daily News* headline of February 4th, 1966: "Court orders Quill and eight to jail today".

John Lawe, as well as being president of Local 100, is International Executive Vice President of the T.W.U. of America, second vice president of the New York City Central Labor Council and a vice president of the New York State AFL-CIO Council. He is also a director of the Hospital Insurance Plan and the MABSTOA Health Benefit Trust.

In 1975, he completed in one year a two-year labour studies course at the New York State School for Industry and Labor at Cornell University and he serves on the Bronx Economic Development Committee.

Democratic Party politics claim some of his time too. In 1978, he was elected a delegate to the party conference in Memphis, Tennessee, by popular vote of his congressional district in Riverdale. In 1984 he was a delegate for the 19th congressional district in San Francisco mandated to vote for Walter Mondale.

It is not surprising that John Lawe is directly concerned in Irish affairs. He has been honoured by Irish Northern Aid and by the Irish National Caucus and he says that the temper of his membership is that "the fight must be kept up. I know there is a multiplicity of Irish organisations, but we are a most difficult race to solidify. We are too weak, too controversial. If we had one organization like the Greeks, the Poles and the Jews have here, our progess would not be so impeded. Jim Delaney's Irish Unity Conference seems to have a better foundation, but then he is a millionaire and he doesn't have to look outside for finance.

"While there is conflict in Ireland there will always be splits in America. That's a fact of life until peace comes by British withdrawal. The Ancient Order of Hibernians is now taking a stronger and more fundamental position, more vocal, keeping up the pressure. I support Noraid and the Caucus. I must give them A for effort. But there seems to be total apathy in Ireland. We shouldn't dictate policy from here, but we become different when we leave home: the agitation will always be here. The present Irish Government has absolutely no credibility with Irish America".

John Lawe is a member of JFK Divison 9 of the A.O.H. and has been honoured by the order. Black, Hispanic and Jewish trade unionists have also heaped honours on him.

His wife, whom he married in 1952, is the former Mary Heaney of Dublin Street, Longford, and they have three children, Desmond, a graduate of Fordham University, is the marketing analyst for the Rockefeller Group which runs the Rockefeller Center in New York; Deirdre, who graduated from Marymount, is a nurse specialist with Survival Technology doing pacemaker monitoring, and Patricia, who went to New York University Medical School and Manhattan College, is now a cardio-vascular product specialist with the Philips North American Medical System.

John Lawe and his family are regular visitors to Ireland, where his brother Bill has developed the home place into a progressive farm. In a recent tribute to a departed colleague, he wrote that "Roosevelt Watts never forgot where he came from". He could have been talking about himself.

Dennis Long

FOR 28 years Anheuser-Busch, Inc., has been the largest brewery in the world. For seven of those years its President has been Dennis Patrick Long. It says much for the unique evolution of America that the descendant of Irish immigrants, who were almost by definition poor, could rise in his own lifetime from office boy to President of a company operating eleven breweries and producing 66 million barrels of beer in a year.

Like the brewery that he loves, Dennis Long is of St. Louis. By an accident of family history, he was born in Chicago, but the Longs are a St. Louis family, and Anheuser-Busch dominates the city which has been called the Gateway to the West.

The brewery that today is the world's greatest almost failed to survive to its fifth birthday. It opened for business in 1852 as Georg Schneider's brewery on the South Side of St. Louis, and within five years was insolvent. Using mainly a loan from Eberhard Anheuser, a group of St. Louis businessmen bought and expanded it until three years later its fortunes flagged again.

Anheuser, who had been born in 1805, had already made a fortune in soap manufacture. He bought up the interests of minority creditors and in 1860 became a reluctant brewer. A year later his daughter Lilly married Adolphus Busch, a young brewery supplier who later became a partner and finally President of the company.

Adolphus Busch, who was born in 1839, is regarded as the founder of the giant industry that he created out of a foundering local brewery. His was the dream of a nation-wide beer appealing to all tastes, and to realise his dream he pioneered a network of railside ice houses to cool rail cars of beer being shipped over long distances, an innovation which about 1877 became the industry's first fleet of refrigerated cars. Pasteurisation ensured the freshness of the beer in transit.

"The King of Beers" is the name given to Budweiser which Busch first made in 1876, using the same ingredients—barley malt, hops and rice—that are used today. Although Budweiser continues to outsell all other brands thoughout the world, it has been joined in the brewery by seven other brands including Michelob, developed in 1896, as "a draft beer for connoisseurs" but since 1961 also sold in bottle. A newcomer in 1984 is LA Brand (Less alcohol for those who want to be more moderate in their consumption of beer).

Strong and sociable, Busch was more than a brewer. He had a natural talent for marketing and public relations and the brewery became a showplace, using only the best horses to pull its delivery wagons and offering visitors a pocket-knife with a peephole through which they could look at a picture of Busch himself.

By 1879, sales had risen to 105,234 barrels and in 1901 the million barrel mark was passed. When Adolphus died in 1913, August A. Busch Sr. took charge. He faced three enormous challenges—the Great War, the Volstead Act which introduced Prohibition, and the Great Depression.

Prohibition was the national experiment in alcohol control which was in force in the United States from 1920 until 1933. It involved an amendment (the 18th) to the Constitution and forbade the manufacture, sale and exchange of intoxicating liquors. Both Houses of Congress passed the Bill against the veto of President Woodrow Wilson and it was ratified by 46 of the 48 states.

A tremendous increase in bootlegging—the illicit traffic in liquor—was the immediate consequence. Smuggling across the Canadian border and by fast motor-boats from ships lying offshore became common; the illicit distillation from sugar and grain became popular. The direct cost to the Government of enforcing Prohibition was $11.6 million in 1928, a figure which should be compared with the collection of $6.1 million in fines against nearly 40,000 people in the same year.

One authority calculated that a single illicit bootleg concern had a chain of 20,000 "speakeasies" where the consumption of alcohol was more or less openly carried on. Prohibition was a plank in Franklin D. Roosevelt's election platform in 1932 and when he won he legalised the sale of 3.2 per cent beer which was available in many States by April 7th, 1933. By November, the Volstead Act was repealed.

The effect of Prohibition on Anheuser-Busch and its President, August Busch, was to make him look to the survival of the company and the jobs it maintained. Going in a series of new directions, he produced corn products, baker's yeast, ice cream, soft drinks, commercial refrigeration units and truck bodies. The company also introduced Bevo, a non-alcoholic malt-derived drink.

All of these products were later discontinued with the exception of baker's yeast, which became a long-term success story beginning in 1927, developing under Adolphus Busch III who became President in 1934, and eventually becoming the national leader in its field.

August A. Busch Jr., who was born in 1899, succeeded his brother Adolphus as President in 1946 and initiated a quite massive expansion. By the time he became Honorary Chairman in 1977, the company had constructed nine branch breweries beginning with Newark, New Jersey, in 1951, and ending with Fairfield, California. Since then the company bought the former Jos. Schlitz Brewing Co. plant outside Baldwinsville, near Syracuse, New York, in 1980. It became fully operational in 1983 and after some expansion in 1984 will have a capacity of 7.2 million barrels a year. August Busch saw sales increase from three million barrels in 1946 to over 34 million barrels in 1974.

Another example of August Busch Jr.'s enterprise was the extension of corporate diversification to include family entertainment, real estate, can manufacturing, transport and major league baseball.

August A. Busch III, who was born in 1937, was elected President in 1974 after 17 years' experience in every major aspect of the business. He became Chief Executive Officer in 1975 and thus was the fourth generation of the family to serve the company in that capacity. In 1977 he was elected Chairman of the Board, introduced five new brands of beer, acquired the country's second largest bakery, opened new family entertainment attractions; extended the company's vertical integration with new can manufacturing and malt production facilities, and diversified further into container recovery, metalised label printing, snackfoods and marketing services. Gross sales increased from $2 billion in 1975 to $6.6 million in 1983.

The restructuring of Anheuser-Busch in 1979 created Anheuser-Busch Companies as the holding company and Anheuser-Busch, Inc., as the brewing organisation, the core business of the vast empire and the one of which Dennis Long has been President since 1977. He and August Busch, his junior by two years as they remind each other on appropriate occasions, have known each other for 20 years.

Long describes himself as "intense, with a bit of insecurity, a great dedication to Anheuser-Busch to which I feel a great obligation because it has been so neat to me. I am responsible for 12,000 people at Anheuser-Busch, Inc., so I have to protect the welfare of say 25,000 people. I have a strong drive to have financial security for my children. I have more than enough to retire on now for myself, but I feel the need to go on for their sake.

"I think we Irish devote our lives more to other people than other races do. I compartmentalise my actions so that my intensity doesn't make me burn out. I don't believe in having a strong social life and my friends are not brewery people. They come from my parish and my love of athletics and especially of soccer, which is one of my releases.

"Whatever community involvement I have has to fit into one of these compartments of my life—family, the Church, soccer, and the brewery. I also periodically decompress with the family. We try to have breakfast in the Sunset Country Club every Sunday if possible. The entire family comes including my nine-month-old grandson Ryan. That is about the only time I use the club, though my house adjoins the fourth green. I have five acres on a golf course and I don't even play".

Dennis Long, a tall handsome man of 49 with silver hair and the most beguiling smile, was made St. Louis Sportsman of the Year in 1984. Soccer is in his blood. His first shoes were soccer shoes. His father's first shoes were soccer shoes. Soccer in St. Louis is 100 years old and the city's soccer park, helped by Anheuser-Busch and promoted by Dennis Long, is probably the finest in the world. Copied from a German complex, it cost $3 million, of which $1 million is underground.

"I am dedicated to soccer in St. Louis", he tells you. "I coached my 18-year old son Patrick through grade school. That was not the optimum way for him, but we won. He was one of the State Champions last year as a junior at Christian Brothers' College High School. This year he made it as a senior and then he quit. What a trauma for this young man—all the peer pressure, the coach pressure, the father pressure. After a week he came back to the game and he is winning, scoring"—and he proudly shows you a cutting from that day's paper.

"Patrick worked here for two summers. He is enamoured of Anheuser-Busch, but I am truly a problem for him. It's difficult being my son. But he does it so well. Patrick's an incredible young man. He wants to go to Rollins College near Orlando in Florida. It's famous for soccer in the European manner".

The brewery plays a remarkable part in the life of Dennis Long's family. His three sisters—Bonnie, Sandy and Doryle—all are married to men working in the brewery. His daughter Tammie at 26 is married to Thomas Werkmeister and his other dauther Kelly Ann, who is 23, is married to Bill Studdard. Both men work at Anheuser-Busch.

Dennis Patrick Long was born in Chicago in 1935, of an Irish American father and a mother of English and French extraction. His father, John J. Long, died in 1972 and his mother, the former Alice Shoults, is now a remarkable 81 years old. An account executive with Standard Oil, his father was made redundant during the Depression and went into the insurance business. When Dennis Long was three years old, the family moved back to St. Louis and his father found work as a labourer in the construction industry. "He soon got fed up with that and became a business agent for his local—Local 110 of the Laborers' Union.

"Life was tough for us", he says. "I had three sisters and two brothers, Kenneth and Terence. I was in the middle. It sounds corny but it's true that we had a poor childhood but an incredible amount of love".

At ten, he was a newsboy; at 14 a grocery clerk. So hard work is no stranger to Long, who started school at St. Columbkille's, went to High School at St. Mary's and studied marketing at night at Washington University in St. Louis. The man's intensity begins to show when it is realised that between the ages of eight and 18 he had 23 wins and only three losses as a boxer and was a high school champion at this sport as well as at soccer, where he was a Missouri champion. (As a soccer coach in 1970 to 1982, he notched up 527 wins against 95 losses in various championships including U.S.A. District and Missouri State).

In 1953, when Dennis Long was 17, he joined Anheuser-Busch as an office boy and elevator operator. "My father told me to do it", he says. "'Find a good solid St. Louis company like the brewery. Go to work', he told me".

In the 31 years since then, he has flown on the wings of the wind. He was 37 when he became Vice President, Non-Beer Products, and that was only five years after he had ceased to lead his own dance band, an enterprise that he kept going for 14 years.

Indeed for eight years in a row, Long had his 14-piece orchestra playing four nights a week; spent 40 hours in the brewery, and did three nights at college.

"You can imagine what a person my wife Barbara is. We lived in a one-bedroomed apartment at the time. She's a marvellous lady, a housewife by choice. We get a rare business trip together but the hub of our existence is our home". Barbara is three-quarters Irish and has traced a Maggie Murphy in her family's background. They met at one of his band engagements.

Being Irish is an important element in the complex being that is Dennis Long. His great grandfather, Bartholomew Long, was born in

1837, possibly in the Dingle area of County Kerry, possibly around Muskerry, County Cork. He died in East St. Louis, Illinois, in June, 1881. He married Mary Sullivan, also possibly from the Dingle Peninsula, certainly from Kerry. She was born in 1845 and died in East St. Louis in June, 1880. Much more than that he does not yet know, but the quest for knowledge is not born of idle curiosity. He has to know. He and Barbara have been to Ireland and met Longs who have offered to help. But the search for his roots is slower than his rise to prominence in Anheuser-Busch.

His Irishness, he feels, has provided some of the qualities that helped to bring him along the road to success. "I feel the strengths I possess can be traced back to a relative from Ireland. If I feel inadequate or get depressed or get down on myself, I remember the Irish blood flowing through my veins and it gives me a new feeling of confidence and strength.

"Considering the problems that we Irish have had for so long and our ability to weather them and to come to such prestigious positions in the United States, I'm very proud of being Irish", he says.

"I know I can get very intense, but we are not without some sense of humour—it's one of the strengths of the Irish people. St. Louis is at least 40 per cent Catholic, a lot of them Irish. My family moved to the Irish Patch in South Side St. Louis when they came here. I still live South. To me South County is home: I like the mix of people in my parish, Our Lady of Providence.

"When I lived in the Irish Patch, 70 per cent of the parish was Irish and I grew up in the atmosphere of a little Ireland. I was an Irish boy soprano, so naturally I had to be a fighter as well". Which is where the boxing came in.

St. Louis lies on the mighty Mississippi surrounded by farms and factories. No one in this city of two million feels that he is far from the land. Dennis Long goes to rural Ireland when he can and already has planned his 1985 visit to Waterford, Killarney and Cork. August Busch lives on a farm and comes to work in the brewery by helicopter every day. "He does not", says Dennis Long, "regard himself as blue blood of St. Louis".

August A. Busch Jr., the Chairman's father, lives on Grant's Farm, a 280-acre estate once owned by Ulysses S. Grant, the Civil War General who became the 18th President of the United States. Grant's Cabin, the only surviving residence hand built by an American President, still stands on the property, which is not only a tourist attraction but adjoins the breeding area and home of the largest herd of Clydesdale horses in the United States.

The world-famous Clydesdale eight-horse hitch is at Anheuser-Busch's St. Louis headquarters. Since 1933, when the company acquired a team of Clydesdales to celebrate the repeal of Prohibition, the fabled hitch with its 2½-ton beer wagon has thundered its way into the hearts of Americans. It was August A. Busch Jr., now Honorary Chairman of the company, who decided in 1933 that a full hitch of these magnificent animals would make a perfect surprise for his father. So on April 7th, 1933, the Budweiser Clydesdale hitch, complete with a brilliant red, white and gold Anheuser-Busch beer wagon designed by Studebaker, was born. Now three teams based in different cities travel 90,000 miles a year to appear in festivals, rodeos, state fairs and of course St. Patrick's Day parades.

Conscious that parts of the St. Louis brewery look like "a pre-Prohibition shoe factory", Dennis Long is engaged on a process of beautification. Part of the process was to spend $800,000 on renovating the 1885 Clydesdale stables, originally built for Mr. Busch's private carriage horses. The attractive new head office building (1981) is by Fred Guyton of Peckham-Guyton, who was the architect of the Busch Gardens theme park at Williamsburg, Virginia.

Major theme parks in Florida and Virginia are operated by the Busch Entertainment Corporation, a diversified operation that features a unique blend of natural beauty and family entertainment activities and attractions. It's a far cry from beer to beauty, one might think, but Anheuser-Busch contains many such surprises, too many to enumerate here, but all a source of pride to President Long, who reminds one that the third modern Olympic Games were held in St. Louis in 1904, during the World's Fair, a paradigm of the continuum and the renewal of leadership that is Anheuser-Busch.

"After Prohibition there were 950 breweries in the United States. Now we are effectively down to five", he says. "The industry is static, yet advertising budgets go up because of competition for a share of the same market. We sold 100 million cases of beer in August of 1984 and we are now brewing in six countries. Indeed when we looked at Ireland we were given a presentation by the Irish Industrial Development Authority that was the most professional we saw in any country; and we are now talking to Brian Slowey and Paddy Galvin of Guinness about the possibility of marketing Budweiser in Ireland".

Dennis Long, Chairman of the Board of Worldwide U.S.O.; board member of half-a-dozen clubs, councils and foundations; recipient of endless awards and medals, still has not been shown the best way in which to demonstrate practical help for Ireland. He is interested in Tony O'Reilly's Ireland Fund; he is a member of the Ancient Order of Hibernians. Yet he says: "If I could only find a proper vehicle . . . . ."

EOIN McKIERNAN

IT is no coincidence that the first Irish symphony commissioned from the United States of America should have been put in train by Dr. Eoin McKiernan and his Irish American Cultural Institute. The institute was looking for a suitable artistic commemoration of the Bicentennial of the American Revolution of 1776. The late Dr. A. J. Potter, voted the most popular Irish composer at the 1970 Festival of 20th Century Music, happily accepted the institute's commission of a work to honour Éamon de Valera as a man who embodied the connection between Ireland and America, a relationship antedating the Revolution but of great significance to it.

One participant in the discussion with Dr. Potter was the then President of Ireland, the late Cearbhall Ó Dálaigh, patron of the Irish American Cultural Institute and an admirer of Potter's genius. The result was *Symphony No. 2: Ireland*, which was completed in the Autumn of 1976. Archie Potter died in July, 1980, a month after seeing his second opera, *The Wedding*, produced at Ireland's National Theatre, the Abbey.

For Eoin McKiernan, President of the Irish American Cultural Institute, man of letters and doer of deeds, such an achievement was all in the day's work—"It isn't a job; it's a mission, seven days a week". The institute, which is the largest Irish organisation in the United States, is based in an old building at the College of St. Thomas in St. Paul, Minnesota, and there he sits with a staff of eight and a worldwide network of members, readers, contacts and friends.

Sits, though, is not an apt word, for Eoin McKiernan has crossed the Atlantic well over 200 times since he first went to Ireland at the age of 15. Those who have had the privilege of interviewing him usually have had to meet him at airport or railway station because he is either on the way to Ireland to hand out funds and awards for Irish artists, poets, writers and musicians, or on the way back to the United States to nurse sponsors and get in the funds to maintain and expand the work of the institute.

One reporter has described McKiernan as "a tall wiry man who would look like Sam Beckett if some photographer had only managed to catch Beckett smiling". He is a gentle persuader, a quiet believer in the gospel of Irish culture. That he has overcome apathy, cynicism and even hostility to breathe life into his dream is a tribute to his determination and fixity of purpose. Only Eoin McKiernan could have cared enough.

"Grace was a great loss to us", says McKiernan, meaning Her Serene Highness Princess Grace of Monaco, who for many years before her untimely death served as International Chairman of the I.A.C.I. It was her idea that the institute's Irish Way programme should be offered to high school students (9th to 11th grade) who every summer get an opportunity to "discover Ireland's hospitality and its ancient, still vital culture; become part of an Irish family, live and learn in Ireland with other American teenagers, and grow by finding out how well they do away from the security of home and friends".

The programme has been going for nine years and has given over 1,000 students a chance to know the real Ireland for nearly six weeks. The reaction of one student from Waterford, Michigan, is typical: "I thought it was the greatest experience of my life. I have gained so much confidence that my whole family notices a huge difference". Indeed more than 75 families have sent at least two of their members on the programme, which in 1984 cost $1,159 plus the air fare and pocket money. Some partial scholarships are available. The criterion is financial need once the selection requirements are met. Each summer the students come from 25 to 30 different states.

Another of McKiernan's many programmes is Irish Perceptions, which continues the I.A.C.I.'s tradition of bringing outstanding lecturers and entertainers from Ireland. Artists, journalists, historians, public figures, writers and musicians have entertained audiences across the States. Recently the participants were Marcus de Búrca, the writer and historian of the Gaelic Athletic Association, the world's largest amateur sports body whose centenary occurs in 1984; Dr. Gearóid Ó Tuathaigh, senior lecturer in modern history at University College, Galway, who lectured on "Cultural Diversity in a Changing Ireland"; Professor Aloys Fleischmann of University College, Cork, composer and founder and conductor of the Cork Symphony Orchestra, and Dáithí Sproule from Derry, the young singer and guitarist, who gave solo performances in Irish and English.

Other cultural imports brought to Americans by courtesy of Eoin McKiernan are professional Irish theatre productions such as Gemini Productions' "I Do Not Like Thee, Doctor Fell" by Bernard Farrell, which toured four states in Autumn, 1982; Irish art and photography exhibitions such as "Ireland and the Irish", mounted by Seamas Daly of Photo Images Ltd. Dublin, which has toured most of the United States and Europe and was seen in Peking and two other Chinese cities in the Summer of 1980; concerts of traditional and classical Irish music; and the Irish Fortnight series which gives an opportunity for Americans to sit down and talk to living Irish scholars, writers and musicians, sometimes in 18 cities with an attendance of 70,000 people.

But for some the greatest achievement wrought by McKiernan is the 19 years' continuous production of *Éire-Ireland*, a quarterly magazine of impeccable standards and consummate interest, devoted to serious scholarly treatment of Irish literature and history. "Aren't you glad there is something Irish that is highbrow?", McKiernan once said with a mischievous grin to a critic who thought the journal was too heavy.

Éire-Ireland goes to every major university in 26 countries in the western world including the Hebrew University of Israel, and embracing Poland as well. McKiernan is the editor and he has as associate editors Henry F. Beechhold and Thomas Dillon Redshaw, and as assistant editors Seán McMahon and Laurence O'Shaughnessy. Together they contrive to make a quarterly book that does great honour to the field of Irish studies.

Academic and scholarly *Éire-Ireland* may be, but there is in it surely a point of contact for everyone with a feeling for good writing and a curiosity about the Ireland we all profess to love. Take the Spring, 1984, table of contents, or some of them. There is "The Art and Politics of the Parnell Monument" by Timothy J. O'Keefe, 20 fascinating pages on a subject which one would have thought, if one thought at all, merited a sentence or two. There is "Energy, Ecstasy, Elegy: Yeats and the Death of Robert Gregory" by Robert Tracy ("...because he was a fighter pilot, Gregory resembled Cuchulain..."). "English Roman Catholics and the Irish Free State in the 1930s" by Thomas R. Greene of Villanova University reaches this conclusion: "On the whole...by the end of the decade Ireland appeared to English Catholics as the last Christian democracy. That view was, in fact, quite a reversal of the one which prevailed at the beginning of the decade". And so on through 160 pages, with incisive book reviews and always a compelling cover design. Where, one wonders, is its equal anywhere? And yet, or as yet, it is largely unsung.

For those of lower brow—and McKiernan knows that not all of the 78,000 members of the I.A.C.I. buy *Éire-Ireland*: "So what"?, he says,

"There are many ways of showing a real genuine interest in Ireland and they are not all scholarly"—there is *Dúchas*, a monthly newsletter or "educational supplement", sent free to all U.S. members. Since 1966, the I.A.C.I. has awarded $10,000 a year in literary prizes, alternately for Irish and English language writers. The 1984 awards went to writers in Irish. Dr. Seán Ó Coileáin was given IR£3,500 for his biography of the poet Seán Ó Riordáin; Liam Ó Muirthile IR£2,500 for his distinguished poetry publications; Micheál Ó hÓdhráin, IR£1,500 for his radio plays for children, and Nollaig Ó Gadhra IR£1,500 for his commentary on contemporary Ireland. Another $10,000 goes to Irish artists every year.

Irish Books and Media, which is run by Eoin McKiernan's daughter Ethna, is the largest supplier of books on Ireland in the United States. She has built it up over seven years to a business with a turnover of $350,000 in 1983 and as well as selling through 200 stores from coast to coast, she is the sole agent for some Irish publishers and a stockist for others. In her own right Ethna McKiernan is a poet of rare insight and honesty. "She would like to write more" says her father, "but the pressure of business is too great".

Ethna Maeve McKiernan is the fourth youngest of Eoin and Jeannette McKiernan's nine children, all of whom have double names. Deirdre Bríd is married in Scottsville, New York, and is busy with wifely, maternal and parochial duties: Kevin Barry is a lawyer by training but a journalist by profession and a Pulitzer nominee; Brendan Colm is a veterinary surgeon with the University of Illinois; the fourth eldest is Nuala Ita, and next to her is Fergus Eoin, a medical doctor in Iowa; after Ethna Maeve comes Grania Bríd, then Gillisa Adeen and the youngest Liadan Mór. "We could have had 18", says Eoin proudly, "if only we had given them single names".

His wife was born Jeannette O'Callaghan from Boston of Irish parents. The O'Callaghan side is from Rathcormac, near Fermoy, County Cork, and her mother was an O'Sullivan from Goleen in West Cork. The first writer of importance to appear in modern Irish was Canon Peter O'Leary, best known for *Séadna*, a novel of 300 pages of the Irish spoken in West Cork when he was a boy. Peter O'Leary, fondly known as *An tAthair Peadar*, taught Irish to Jeannette O'Callaghan's father.

Eoin McKiernan himself was born on Manhattan in 1915 and was four years old when the family moved upstate to a small town on the Hudson River called Cold Spring. There were no amenities there. "I remember when the toilet came, and we had paraffin lamps until later the electricity was laid on. My father was working on a new waterworks to supply New York City, and he became foreman. There were 75 children in the village school and there was a railway. We were poor. There were four of us and our parents, and our biggest excitement was a long family walk.

"My father was born in Manhattan, youngest of an immigrating family, and my mother was from County Clare. From her I learned Irish songs and stories in the style of Éamon Kelly. I was the eldest and I knew every pishogue or folkbelief that she could pass on, though the only Irish she had was some songs and prayers.

"My Mother never tried to make us Irish, but the fact that we lived in the country in a small place made us different from the Irish in the city. My father died when I was 12 and it was decided that I should go to Ireland, but I already had the advantage of a rural upbringing. My feet were mired in the bog at Tullygavan West near Lahinch, County Clare, and I learned from my grandmother a fund of stories and folklore that is with me still. I didn't go to school there but I learned to speak Irish in Rosmuc in Connemara" (where Patrick Pearse's cottage is still preserved and open to the public).

"My family moved back to Manhattan from Cold Spring when my father died, and I soon joined them and went to the Cathedral College and then to St. Joseph's, where I did a B.A. in English and Classics. I did my master's in Education at the University of New Hampshire and taught for some years until I got a Ph.D. in English from Penn State University. Years later, Ireland honoured me with a D. Litt. from the National Univerity.

"A degree in the depression did not get you a job, so I worked with Macy's as a junior executive for a couple of years. I was living in Palisades, New York, and I found my work fairly exciting. Macy's at the time had five divisions, one of them being management, and that's where I ended up, in charge of 700 employees.

"I left Macy's because I had a hankering to live in Ireland (I was married in 1938). Instead I went farming in New Hampshire and right through the war I was manager of a 1,000-acre farm. I did not amass enough capital to go home. There was no way I could get a farm in Ireland.

"When I gave up farming, I taught English for a while at a secondary school in New Hampshire and then I got an appointment at the State University of New York at Genesco. The area was dominated by a long-established, you might say patrician family. They used to foxhunt and had lived in a baronial style for 200 years, when they owned all the land for 30 miles around. Over the years they had imported gardeners from Ireland. To them a professor of English was a welcome guest.

"My wife Jeanette, whom I met when I was 16, always says that from the first day she met me I was pushing for an Irish American Cultural Institute. At any rate in 1957, which to me is a key date in my life, I was invited as chairman of a national committee of the National Council of Teachers of English to speak at a convention in Minneapolis. I had all the myopia of an East Coast Irishman, but I gave a talk and I met the President of St. Thomas's College in St. Paul. We talked about Ireland until 3 o'clock in the morning, and some months later I got an invitation from him to head up the English Department at St. Thomas's.

"That man was James P. Shannon, who later became a Bishop and later still got married. He has written a book on Irish settlements in the Mid-West which was published by Yale.

"Shannon's invitation was in generous terms. He said we should fly out to St. Paul, all expenses paid, and spend a week to see if we liked it. We were impressed and took the job—but I stipulated that I wanted 12 months in Ireland first. So we all went to Ireland and the children went to University College Dublin, to Muckross Park College (we lived in Donnybrook) and to Oatlands College. That was in 1959–60.

"I had been in Ireland during de Valera's election campaign in 1932 and met him then. We got on famously and in his later years as President of Ireland I always had access to Áras an Úachtaráin in the Phoenix Park. When he was retired in 1973 and living in Talbot Lodge nursing home, I could go to see him any time I arrived.

"Because of my intimate knowledge of Ireland, I was always interested in all kinds of inter-cultural developments, and especially in the Experiment in International Living, who were sending groups of American students anywhere but to Ireland. I became a member of the board and was able to influence them to send people to Ireland from about 1954 on.

"My year in Ireland was an opportunity to carry the message of cultural relations further. I went to see Brendan O'Regan of Shannon Development to determine whether he would back Muckross House as a staging centre for all the 2,000 Experiment in International Living people who went to Europe every year. I couldn't persuade anybody—

not Shannon Development, not the Tourist Board nor Aer Lingus. Ireland could have become the broker for all these trips but the powers that be couldn't see it.

"These Experiment in International Living people were the most prestigious in this country. Many of them came from Ivy League colleges. I had many talks with de Valera about my ideas and especially about the need for a cultural institute with a foot in each country to act as a conduit.

"I came back to St. Paul in August, 1960, the concept still simmering in my mind. So in 1962, when I was in my mid-40s, I decided: right, I've got to show them what I mean, and two years later we set up the institute which is still going full strength.

"At that time the Germans, the Poles, the Jews were all looking into their past history and universities were offering courses in ethnic studies. But the Irish American community was dying on the vine when my wife and I and Patrick Butler (who made his money in iron ore) decided to plan the institute.

"During 1962 to 1964 I prepared and presented a 53-episode television series on aspects of Ireland which was shown all over the States. We got over 30,000 letters as a result, expressing further interest and this, using those names and addresses asking for a $10 subscription, was our chance to float the institute. Only four or five TV stations took the first series which Patrick Butler paid for. But the second was shown on 46 stations under the title 'Irish Diary'. Patrick Butler financed them too.

"Among the letters we got was one from a woman in Seattle who said (McKiernan's eyes well up with tears): 'I hated the Irish all my life until I saw your programmes'. Another women in Boston wrote in a lovely hand: 'You've done so much for my soul. I was a domestic servant with more culture than the people I worked for. To them I was only Irish. The series was balm to my heart'.

"We are now the strongest Irish organisation in this country and we have been able to award a total of $400,000 to the arts in Ireland without receiving a penny of State money. So many people here have an interest in Ireland but want no part of what I call the Green sickness, or our annual bout of Paddywhackery. They are the people who have made it possible for us to raise $2.5 million in the last two years.

"But money is not the problem. We're only scratching at the surface of what could be done. Trade, tourism, investment will all suffer from Ireland's neglect of the resource America represents. Most of all

Ireland's voice in the world will be no more than an insignificant whisper. The 44 million who claimed Irish origins in the last U.S. Census is a meaningless figure. If we had one million caring Irish Americans we could accomplish something.

"The average age of the Irish immigrant is about 60. Our quota is low and last year saw only about 700 emigrate. So the only way to maximise an Irish impression on America is through cultural programmes. Yet it's only quite recently that the Government appointed a cultural attaché to the Embassy here and the Embassy's budget is quite inadequate.

"I don't want to talk about a grand scheme until I can deliver, but having discussed an assessment of the situation and a well-planned offensive on a broad front with three Taoiseachs, I'm delighted that we seem to be entering the home straight. Our greatest contribution to date is an effective and sophisticated presentation of truly cultured programmes over a wide area in the States—and we have only scratched the surface".

Whatever his master plan is, Eoin McKiernan can be counted on to make it work. Indeed as he approaches 70 and is actively seeking someone who will carry on his life's work, it would be a fitting climax to a career in pursuit of excellence if the Irish America to which he has given so much were to reward him in return with a triumphal tribute to his tenacity.

T. Kevin Mallen

"THE American Irish Foundation", wrote *The Irish Times* in August 1974, "has selected Thomas Kilroy (the playwright and novelist) as the recipient of its bounty this year . . . . . The prize is also evidence that the Irish in the United States are doing something to help the culture of the mother country". In that year the President of the American Irish Foundation was T. Kevin Mallen, a native of County Wicklow, long-serving businessman in various countries in Asia, and outstanding entrepreneur and philanthropist in San Francisco.

Founded in 1963 by President John F. Kennedy of the United States and President Éamon de Valera of Ireland, the Foundation has a distinguished record of discriminating grant aiding. In Kevin Mallen's year alone, it made a gift of over 600 United States legal volumes to the Library of the King's Inns in Dublin; a grant to the Young Writers' Workshop, part of Writers' Week in Listowel, County Kerry, and a third annual gift to the Killarney Bach Festival. Under the leadership of John D.J. Moore, then U.S. Ambassador to Ireland, a beginning was made towards the establishment of a chair of American Studies at University College, Dublin.

In addition, the Foundation continued its support of the project to catalogue the papers of the O'Conor family of Clonalis by Professors Gareth and Janet Dunleavy of the University of Wisconsin, a project which ten years later has come to fruition. St. Michael's House in Dublin, which serves the mentally retarded, was the beneficiary of money for its research programme, and other projects being promoted were the microfilming of the papers of Ernie O'Malley, the War of Independence and Civil War leader, and the papers of General Richard Mulcahy, who fought against O'Malley in the Civil War of 1922–23.

What is remarkable about Kevin Mallen's work as President is the diversity of his activity and the strength of the support that the Foundation could muster, then as now. At the presentation of the library volumes in the King's Inns were the then Taoiseach, Liam Cosgrave; Mr. Justice Brian Walsh of the Supreme Court; the Irish member of the European Court and soon to be President of Ireland, Cearbhall Ó Dálaigh; a former Taoiseach, the late John A. Costello,

Senior Counsel; Ambassador John D.J. Moore of the United States, and President T. Kevin Mallen of the American Irish Foundation.

Mr. Justice Walsh, acknowledging the gift as being of immense value to the Library and the members of Ireland's legal profession, noted specifically that "the area of constitutional rights has become remarkably similar in the Irish and United States courts, particularly in the last 20 years, and the decisions of the United States courts are a source not only of interest but also of encouragement to the judiciary of Ireland".

The Secretary to the American Irish Foundation in 1974 was William V. Shannon, then on the editorial board of the *New York Times*, later to become a hardworking and widely admired U.S. Ambassador to Ireland, and now a professor at Boston University and still a director of the Foundation, as are Michael J. Dargan of the large Irish company Cement Roadstone; Niall Crowley, Chairman of Allied Irish Banks; Peter Dailey, the former U.S. Ambassador to Ireland; Robert F. Kane, his successor; Tadhg O'Sullivan, the present Irish Ambassador to the United States, and Kevin Mallen himself, among many others including Mrs. Michael Smurfit of the Jefferson Smurfit Company, Mrs. Anna McGrath, wife of Paddy McGrath of Waterford Glass, and John A. Mulcahy of Bronxville, New York, and Waterville, County Kerry.

On the National Committee of the Foundation can be found such outstanding people as James Cummins of Cummins Building, Inc., in San Francisco; J. Peter Grace, Chairman of W.R. Grace and Company, New York, and Éamon Keegan of Becker Paribas in San Francisco, as well as two distinguished Irish Americans who form part of this book—James A. (Jim) Delaney, President of the Rand Development Corporation in San Antonio, Texas; and John P. (Jack) Dunfey of the Dunfey Hotels Corporation, Hampton, New Hampshire.

Altogether, the American Irish Foundation constitutes a formidable force for good in the development of cultural and environmental relations between the United States and Ireland, and the man from Grangecon in County Wicklow has played no small part in its growth. The current president, John J. Brogan of Palm Beach, Florida, and Chatham, Massachusetts, is a trustee of several foundations including that of the Gregorian University of Rome, Italy.

He succeeded A.W.B. (Billy) Vincent of San Francisco and Killarney, County Kerry, who has become Chairman of the Board. Billy Vincent, who deserves a chapter to himself, is the son of Arthur Rose

Vincent, who received Muckross Estate as a wedding present from his father-in-law, William Bourn, and after his wife's death presented the entire demesne to the Irish nation in 1933, thus adding the Bourn-Vincent Memorial Park and Muckross House to the treasures of Killarney. Arthur Rose Vincent is said to have been buried standing up in Killegy churchyard, looking out over the lakes he loved.

Thomas Kevin Mallen was born in 1905 to the master of Grangecon National School and his wife, also a teacher. Grangecon is a tiny village near the town of Baltinglass, County Wicklow, and there the Mallons raised nine boys and a girl. (The spelling of Mallon with an "e", was a mistake by the Registrar of Births, Marriages and Deaths).

Kevin Mallen's father came from Carbery in County Kildare. His grandfather was a "hedge schoolmaster", running one of the peripatetic schools that were conducted in the open at a time when there was no other form of instruction for the children of "the men of no property", as Wolfe Tone called them. The Mallons came originally from Dungannon, County Tyrone. Kevin Mallen's mother was from Dublin and had taught at the highly reputable Mount Anville convent school in Dundrum, County Dublin, before she married about 1890.

The Mallen children first attended their parents' school, to which Kevin's father was appointed in January, 1888. It is instructive to read the report of Mr. McDonnell, the District Inspector of Schools, for November, 1886, and to compare his comments with those he made two years later.

In 1886, he wrote in his precise longhand: "Thirty three pupils were presented for examination, and of these nine were presented a third time, and three a second time, in the same classes. In first and second classes very few of the children were able to read or spell the easiest lessons in their books; and in third, fourth and fifth classes there was barely a trace of Grammar or of Geography. Altogether the school is one of the most worthless I have ever examined . . . . ".

When Mr. McDonnell visited Grangecon on November 5th, 1888, he was able to report: "Since Mr. Mallon's appointment in January last, the school has made very satisfactory progress in numbers, tone and efficiency. The junior classes are well prepared but the senior classes are not yet up to the standard in several subjects. Order and discipline are good, and the tone of the school high. The school room is in good order, and extremely clean and neat, and choice flowers, which the children look after, are growing in the windows. Altogether I was much pleased . . . . . Needlework is very well taught by Miss Mallon".

Six of the Mallen boys were sent to Rockwell College near Cashel, County Tipperary. Kevin went there in 1919 and found the food "awful" after the Great War. That war had seen his brother Bill killed in action in France in 1917 by the same shell that killed the saintly Jesuit Father Willie Doyle. Bill was in the Dublin Fusiliers: Father Willie was chaplain to the 8th Royal Irish Fusiliers.

By another extraordinary coincidence, three of Kevin Mallen's brothers died in 1984: Seán, who was a civil servant in the Customs and Excise service; Kieran, known as "KC" because his second name was Colman, who was a distinguished surgeon in the Royal Army Medical Corps and in Weston super Mare, Somerset, England, was a fellow of the Royal College of Surgeons in Ireland and of the British Medical Association: he was awarded an M.B.E.; and Maurice, who was a pharmacist in Dublin, died within months of each other in a tragic year. His brother Brendan who is a doctor living in Weston super Mare, is not enjoying robust health.

Also in early 1984, one of Kevin Mallen's closest friends, Martin Gleeson, who had been Chief Executive Officer of the City of Dublin Vocational Education Committee, died. Gleeson's parents were the teachers in the National School in the neighbouring village of Stratford-on-Slaney, where from 1785 to 1850 cotton and linen printing were carried on, giving work for up to 1,000 people. The village was laid out and built for Henry Stratford who became Earl of Aldborough in 1777 and provided houses and bleach greens for a cotton factory, built a church and chapel, and encouraged settlers.

By 1922, when the Civil War began, Kevin Mallen says: "I was known as the only Free Stater in Rockwell", the majority of the boys siding with the insurgent Republicans. But he met Éamon de Valera, Cathal Brugha and Seán MacBride in Rockwell about Easter, 1922, before Brugha was killed in the burning ruins of the Hammam Hotel in O'Connell Street, Dublin. J. Bowyer Bell has put the resulting end of I.R.A. resistance in the city thus: "Put on the defensive at once, cut off from reinforcements, without artillery or armoured cars, the I.R.A. re-ran the reel of 1916".

One consequence of the Civil War was that the universities were closed, so Kevin Mallen joined the fledgling Air Corps, of which the adjutant was Colonel Éamon (Ned) Broy. Broy in 1933 was to replace the dismissed General Eoin O'Duffy as Commissioner of the Garda Síochána, the unarmed police force. Broy recruited a new "S-branch" made up of former I.R.A. men, fully armed, who immediately were nicknamed the Broy Harriers after a well-known pack of hounds which was hunted around the area of Bray, County Wicklow.

Another colleague of Kevin Mallen's in the Air Corps was Larry Stanley, the legendary Kildare Gaelic footballer. Colonel Broy wanted to establish Irish classes at the air base; Mallen wore the gold *fáinne* or ring of the Gaelic League, "so Broy gave me 37 shillings and sixpence a week and I taught until I became quartermaster at Baldonnel airfield in 1925".

The Civil Service was opening up for bright young men as British members departed, so Mallen joined the Land Commission under Judicial Commissioner the Hon. Mr. Justice Wylie. It was an exciting time in a department of State that now has run its course. The Minister for Agriculture, Paddy Hogan, had introduced the 1923 Land Act which provided for the completion of land purchase and reduced rents. One of the three Commissioners was Kevin R. O'Shiel, barrister-at-law, whose daughter, Eda O'Shiel Sagarra, is now Professor of German at Trinity College, Dublin.

At the Land Commission, Mallen's mentor was Inspector Edward Richardson "who took me under his wing until he became inadvertently involved in a dispute and left the service after advising me that I should leave too. I was captain of the Dublin Boat Club at the time and I joined the Gestetner company in 1928.

"I did very well with Gestetner and they sent me to Singapore for 18 months. Then they appointed a Gestetner agency in the Philippines in 1931 and I became their office equipment manager. The firm also held an IBM agency. I saw pretty quickly that the wagon to hitch my star to was IBM and I made my first visit to America in 1934 to see IBM in New York. They asked me to open an IBM office in Manila".

The Philippines is where he met his future wife. Jane Rice, whom he describes as "an Army brat", was born in the Philippines in 1910 when her father was G-3 of the U.S. Army there. She graduated in biochemistry at the University of Utah and was engaged to marry a Mormon in Salt Lake City when Mallen's friend Floyd McCarthy spotted her at the Army and Navy Club in Manila and said to Mallen: "Bet you wouldn't throw that girl in the pool". They were married in 1935 and in December, 1940, Mallen sent his family home because he could see the war coming.

He himself left the Philippines on November 17th, 1941, on the last boat before Pearl Harbour. Six days after the Japanese attack, he reached Hawaii and by Christmas he had rejoined Jane, whose father was by now Commanding Officer of Fort McDowell on Angel Island in San Francisco Bay.

"I still had my Irish papers", he says, "and I went to Washington and since I wanted to help I was commissioned into the U.S. Army and appointed to the Military Intelligence Division of the War Department". As Chief of the South-East Asia branch covering Burma and Thailand Mallen went with an Air Commando outfit to support General Wingate's Chindits in Burma. His "loyalty and devotion to duty" as Lt.-Col.Thomas K. Mallen are acknowledged by the War Department and in a Presidential Citation.

When the war was over in 1945, Mallen went back to IBM and was appointed General Manager for the Far East with responsibilities from Tokyo to New Zealand and from Hawaii to the Philippines. "There were no jet planes then, so flying great distances was hard because you were frequently fogbound or stormbound".

T.J. Watson, whose eponymous son has just retired from the board, was the "boss" of IBM. "He and I used to squabble occasionally and he'd say to me: 'Don't get your Irish up, Mr. Mallen'. Everybody was Mister to him. He was a truly wonderful man whose vision and integrity built IBM into the magnificent company it is today".

In 1949, Kevin Mallen left IBM to become a partner in Ayala Associates in San Francisco. Among their holdings was a controlling interest in Ampex, then a fledgling in San Carlos. Mallen simultaneously became Executive Vice President and General Manager, becoming Chairman of the Board from 1953 to 1956. This sound and video company began with 13 people in 1948 and now employs 8,000 people worldwide. It is one of the world's great success stories and Kevin Mallen obviously relishes the part he played in it.

In 1961, when he was 56, he joined Sutro and Co. Incorporated, a securities investment firm established on the West Coast since 1858. The firm, of which he is Vice President, is predominantly Jewish—"the best people in San Francisco", he says, citing his friend Mayor Diane Feinstein as an example. Twenty-four years later, he still attends the office on California Street two days a week and spends the rest of his time in Palo Alto, where he lives and has an office.

Kevin and Jane Mallen have six daughters. Wendy is married to the President of his own microchip company and has a daughter who graduated from the University of California in San Diego in June, 1984.

Patricia lives with her husband in Venezuela. Their two daughters graduated in 1984, one from the University of California at Davis, the other from the College of Notre Dame at Belmont. Janny, who recently spent four weeks in a coma after a car crash, has two boys. Margie is a business girl, and her younger sister Terry (Therese) lives in the Sierras. The youngest, Seana, is a well-known and successful artist in Santa Cruz and "is a character out of a book. When she puts her hat on, her house is thatched", says Kevin Mallen fondly.

A member of the Board of Trustees of the University of San Francisco for the past 20 years, Mallen is also Trustee of the College of Notre Dame, Belmont, California. One of his greatest interests was the Peninsular Symphony Orchestra. Jane's major concern was the Community Association for the Retarded in Palo Alto, where the now famous Respite House was established in her honour. Opera, symphony, ballet, restaurants—San Francisco has them all. "I know nowhere better to live".

Years ago, Kevin Mallen bought Seymour Heatley's Churchtown House near Dublin. When the Dublin County Council got a compulsory purchase order for the house in order to use the land for public housing, Mallen in turn offered the mansion to the government to use as a Prime Minister's residence or for whatever purpose they saw fit. Seán Lemass, the Taoiseach of the day (1959–1966) declined Mallen's offer and when he was pleading with the builder, the late Matt Gallagher, at least to preserve some trees, Gallagher's response was to look round him and say: "All I can see is roofs and roofs". "Well, Matt", said Mallen, "I'm sorry for you".

He bought Priorsland in Carrickmines, County Dublin, where later his neighbours were Charles Acton, the Music Critic of *The Irish Times*, and his wife Carol. But the imposition of the new Wealth Tax made him sell Priorsland, which had been the home of T.V. Murphy, the Chairman of Independent Newspapers. Mallen now uses his cottage at nearby Ballyogan for his thrice-yearly visits to Ireland, where he finds his "pals are dying off".

"You can't avoid roots", he says. "Jane finds it hard to understand. For example, the Macnamara family of Corofin, County Clare, were still friends because one of them, Michael, was in the Free State Army with me".

He retains a deep interest in the destiny of Northern Ireland and says Seán Donlon, now Secretary of the Department of Foreign Affairs and formerly Irish Ambassador to the United States, has been a good friend to the American Irish Foundation.

His philosophy of life he sums up in a sentence: "A reputation for integrity and decency is the most important thing in life".

THOMAS E. MORAN

AT 0940 hours on February 22nd, 1984, the Chinese ro/ro carrier *Gu Bei Kou* sailed from Berth 64 of the Maher Terminal in Port Elizabeth, New Jersey, bound for China on the first of the China Ocean Shipping Company's fortnightly direct service from the United States to China.

On the same day and month in 1784, the American sailing ship *Empress of China* set sail from New York under the command of Captain John Green to become the first vessel to arrive in China under American colours. She carried a cargo of ginseng, a medicinal root found in New England, and pelts. Six months later, on August 23rd, 1784, the 350-ton ship arrived in Macao before navigating 70 miles of the Pearl River to Whampoa Anchorage and Canton.

The *Empress of China* returned to New York in 1785 with a cargo of teas, silks, spices and the first Chinese fans to reach the United States. These fans, now priceless treasures, became the fashion in 19th-century America.

Two hundred years later, the *Gu Bei Kou* carried a variety of containerised general cargo, break bulk cargo and large roll on/roll off cargo. Built in 1980, the 14,000-ton carrier was seen off from New York harbour by Captain-Pilot Raymond Poissant of the tug *Carol Moran*, one of the huge fleet of tugboats and other vessels owned by the Moran Towing and Transportation Company, Inc.

Thomas E. Moran is the President of Moran Towing and Transportation, a company founded in 1860 and still wholly owned by the Moran family. Although it is one of the largest tugboat companies in the world, the company's sales and earnings are a closely guarded secret. Indeed the latest figures released were in 1944 when it had revenues of $8 million and its 50 tugs each had a profit of $50 to $75 a day. Now there are 75 to 80 tugboats sailing every country; 20 ocean barges of 20-30,000 tons carrying cargoes such as Moroccan wheat, and subsidiary companies operating from Maine to Texas with the emphasis more firmly on transport than towing.

"I feel very strongly about my Irish roots", says Tom Moran. Lying on the table in his office on the 53rd floor of the World Trade Center, with a spectacular view of the river and its tugboats with a large M painted on the funnel, is a copy of "Irish Americans in Business".

His great grandfather, Michael Moran, was a boy in Kill Lara, County Westmeath, when his parents, exhausted by the Great Famine of 1846-48, took ship from Liverpool in 1849 for New York. Michael's mother, Mary Moran, died on the voyage and he and his father Thomas settled in Frankfort, New York, where they had cousins who took them in.

Michael Moran was 18 when he began to work as a mule skinner on the Erie Canal, which was completed in 1825 to connect Lake Erie at Buffalo with the Hudson River at Albany and Troy, a distance of 363 miles. The mule skinner's job was to beat the mules who pulled the canal-barges from the towpath. The Erie was a very important commercial link because it opened up the Mid-West of America to Europe, and Michael Moran took the opportunity to get to know the people living on the barges, many of them poor Irish who had made their way to Brooklyn to escape the Famine.

Tom Moran quotes the inscription on the Statue of Liberty, now cut into a stone at John F. Kennedy Airport as well:

Give me your tired, your poor
Your huddled masses, yearing to
breathe free
Send these, the homeless, tempest-tost
to me
I lift my lamp beside the
golden door

"Michael Moran was personable and ambitious and because they were a cut above the barge people he listened to the friends who said: 'Mike, you should come to the big city and see if you cannot make a go of the tugboat business'".

So in 1860, with $2,700 he had saved from his mule skinning, he rented a tugboat by the day. Moran grew up with New York and the company's history is as tough and colourful as the city's. When he began, a steamer from Europe pulling into the Narrows caused the tugboat skippers to scramble for the business on a first-come first-served basis. Bloody dockside brawls were commonplace, as were epic drinking sessions at which the captain who stayed on his feet knew that the next ship to come in would be his.

In spite of fierce—sometimes literally cut-throat—competition, the Moran tugs with the while capital M on their funnels stayed ahead in the water, manned by the brains as well as the brawn of the family. Michael Moran was the instigator of a Towboat Exchange which parcelled out the work among the owners. A photograph of him, with white mutton-chop whiskers, bowler hat, velvet-collared coat and gold watch-chain, was taken in 1888 at 140 Broad Street or possibly South Street in the middle of 25 of his colleagues. He died in 1904.

Tom Moran's father, Edmond J. Moran, is Michael Moran's great nephew. He is 87 now and headed the firm from 1939 to 1964. He was not at the helm when Moran tugs docked the French Atlantic liner *Normandie* on her maiden voyage in 1935, but he supervised her departure for Newark eleven years later when she was cut up for scrap.

In his time Edmond Moran towed Texas towers to offshore oil stations, huge dredgers to the East Indies, oil derricks to Maracaibo and, in an incident that made St. Lawrence Seaway lock-keepers shake their heads in disbelief, brought a 26-foot-wide tugboat, the *Pauline L. Moran* with a 23-foot-wide submarine lashed alongside her through the 43-foot locks. The trick was that the bulge in the tugboat's side nestled above the underwater bulge of the submarine, leaving a tidy six inches to spare. (All the tugs carry the names of members of the family).

In the Second World War, Edmond Moran became a rear-admiral who under Admiral Harold Stark was in charge of the Mulberry Harbour operation in Normandy on D-day plus one. He was awarded the C.B.E. (Commander of the British Empire) in 1945.

"I'm the fourth generation of hard-working businessmen", says Tom Moran. He is the eldest of six and his younger brother, Edmond J. Moran Jr., was last year appointed manager of the Moran Barge Division in New York. Before that, he directed Moran Maritime Services, Inc., in Houston, Texas. Among the Moran company's overseas agents is the Leinster Shipping Company Ltd. in Dublin.

Tom Moran left high school in Portsmouth, Rhode Island, where he was in the care of the Benedictine Fathers. He was 19 and he went to sea for 2½ years, during the war in the Merchant Marine, "all over the islands of the Pacific, in New Guinea and the Philippines". After working for a steamship company, he joined Moran in 1964. He was a member of the National Defense Executive Reserve, and it is ironic that the sole survivor on the U.S. East Coast of the 2,700 Liberty ships built during World War II was towed in 1983 to the Maritime Administration's James River reserve fleet in Virginia on the hawser of the *Amy*

Moran. The *John W. Brown* had served for decades as a schoolship for the New York Board of Education and as a well-known landmark in the city. When she first arrived in 1946, she berthed at East River piers before moving to the west side of Manhattan where her "second career" ended when the Board of Education transferred its maritime trades programme to new shoreside facilities in June, 1982.

While hundreds of high school students seeking maritime careers were grateful for her shipboard environment, the *John W. Brown* also attracted the attention of the general public as a World War II veteran. Now a John W. Brown Preservation Society has been formed by the National Maritime Historical Society and the ship has been designated a Merchant Marine Memorial by Act of Congress signed by President Ronald Reagan. Her "third career" is beginning.

The third career of Thomas E. Moran has lasted a long time. In the family business which he heads, nobody loses sight of the family traditions of toughness and independence. Moran Towing and Transportation enjoys no Government subsidies and has never sought help in meeting its foreign competition. As Admiral Edmond Moran said in 1962: "We put our own money in it, and we fight as hard as we can".

Tom Moran, who has made several business visits to Dublin and Cork, is married (his second marriage) to a Kirkwood whose parents were Boston Catholics of Northern Ireland extraction. He has five children and eight grandchildren and enjoys a game of golf in his home town, New Canaan, Connecticut.

Almost a century and a quarter old, Moran's company is still the world leader in the tugboat and ocean barge business. Under his astute leadership, it is set fair to stay ahead in the business that the young man from County Westmeath founded in the Port of New York all those years ago.

It is fitting for the descendants of an Irish emigrant that the Statue of Liberty, symbol of hope and freedom to so many of Ireland's poor huddled masses, should be ready to celebrate its centenary in 1986.

JOSEPH M. MURPHY

JOSEPH M. Murphy is different. Unlike most Irish Americans whom one meets in the course of researching a book of this kind, he stumbled late on his roots and found them in response to a perceived need to know where he had come from. President of Drexel Burnham Lambert Realty Inc. and President of the Lambert Brussels Corporation, Joe Murphy is the archetype of the self-made man who says: "I made my first million by the age of 35. Only in America can that happen".

Drexel Burnham Lambert Realty Inc. is the real-estate arm of the Wall Street brokerage and investment banking house Drexel Burnham Lambert Group Inc. which in January, 1984, was described in an analysis of the top 15 underwriters by *Investment Dealers Digest* in these terms: "The real shocker is the all around performance of Drexel, which edged its way up from number eight in 1982 with $2.271 billion in deals it lead managed to number six by more than tripling its dollar volume to $7.650 billion".

It was William Greene, President in the 1930s of the American Federation of Labour, who was surprisingly unenthusiastic about measures to help the unemployed. "The real remedy for unemployment", he said, "is employment". Nowadays Wall Street articulates its role in job formation in simple terms:

"The process of economic growth through change is fuelled by capital, and capital markets are the life-support system of a free economy. Wall Street channels and rechannels capital toward firms investors believe will use it most effectively and away from firms they believe will not. It is forever revising these estimates.

"There are few human activities that seem, on the surface, to be more chaotic and irrational than the daily madness of a trading floor. But is is here that masses of information are translated into the common language of price—the clear, calibrated signals which guide the continuous deployment and redeployment of the economy's capital resources". The words are from Drexel Burnham Lambert's annual review of 1983. The sentiments are the essence of capitalism which works, as Adam Smith wrote in 1776, as if it were guided by an invisible hand.

The real estate activities of Drexel Burnham Lambert trace their origins to the late 1960s with the entry of Groupe Bruxelles Lambert SA into the United States real estate market. This Belgian-based financial holding company with total assets of over $30 billion at first focused its sights on the lodging or hotel industry because of the excellent potential returns. In 1976 the group became a major investor in Drexel Burnham and Co., creating the Drexel Burnham Lambert Group and then forming Drexel Burnham Lambert Realty which today, under the Presidency of Joe Murphy, is a diversified real estate investment organisation offering a wide range of products and services to a vast array of domestic and international clients.

With six regional offices, over 50 parent company offices and a real estate portfolio valued at $300 to $400 million, the company covers the four phases of investment—acquisition, management, refinancing and disposition.

As well as being President of the realty company since 1976, Joe Murphy is President of the Lambert Brussels Corporation, which is 53 per cent owned by Groupe Bruxelles Lambert S.A. He is responsible for the U.S. operations of the group, the second largest private financial group in Belgium, of which he is a Director and member of the Executive Committee. Lambert Brussels, which ranks high in the esteem of Baron Lambert, Chairman of the Board of Groupe Bruxelles Lambert, was launched in August, 1983, and like Drexel Burnham Lambert Realty, has its headquarters in that masterpiece of Art Deco, the Chrysler Building on Lexington Avenue.

The keystone of the whole organisation, Burnham and Company, was erected in 1935 by I.W. Burnham II who only in March, 1984, stepped down from the Chairmanship of Drexel Burnham Lambert to become Honorary Chairman and to be succeeded by Robert E. Linton, who is also Chief Executive Officer. Joe Murphy is a member of the parent firm's powerful Executive Committee.

One of Joe Murphy's more colourful operations is his role as Managing General Partner of Ocean Club, a 725-unit condominium development in Atlantic City, New Jersey, the reborn city which since 1978 has begun to rival Las Vegas as the casino capital of the U.S. Built to an ambitious design by Californian architect David Jacobson Jr. who has already worked on the Sands, Claridge and Harrah's Trump and Hilton hotel casinos, Ocean Club will be the most expensive residential highrise on the East Coast from New York to Miami.

A $122 million construction loan from Bank of America was

negotiated by Murphy, who is a private investor in the twin-tower 34-storey project due for completion in the fall of 1984—"$200 million of building in one city block", as one partner enthuses. And the price tag? For an apartment, $180,000; for a penthouse duplex, a shade over $1 million. And long before the builders move out, the buyers are clamouring to move in. "Joe Murphy's Law", one magazine called it two years ago, and certainly it is a large and positive contribution to Atlantic City's need for more residential accommodation.

Pavarini Construction of Connecticut are general contractors for Ocean Club. They were the builders of the new wings for the Metropolitan Museum of Art in New York, the architect of which was Kevin Roche.

Who buys a condo on the beach in Atlantic City? A lot of doctors and other professional people, Al Gardner the resident partner says. "They are the nouveaux riches who like to have fun with their money and yet they're not the high rollers. Most people are buying as investments or second homes. It's the typical Atlantic City situation—stay here part of the year, and rent the rest of the time". And there are artists and entertainers like Vic Damone, Rod McKuen, Leroy Neiman, David Brenner and Art Linkletter who play the casino showrooms.

As President of Drexel Burnham Lambert Realty, Murphy has also been responsible for $180 million of financing for Golden Nugget; $90 million for Tropicana and $40 million for the Playboy Hotel and Casino, among many other Atlantic City financings.

But Atlantic City is only one place in one state in one country. Joe Murphy spends a lot of time in New York and a lot of time in Brussels, where boardroom discussions are in French. His impeccable blue pin-stripe suit and well-groomed silver hair belie the man "whose pen", as one reporter put it, "could command dollars far beyond most of our wildest dreams", but who on the building site can be seen unwrapping a ham sandwich from the local delicatessen.

Joseph Michael Murphy was born 49 years ago in the Inwood section of Washington Heights, New York. As he grew up, there was lots of greenery and it was "a nice city to live in as cities go". His father, who died in 1964, was the only brother of five to emigrate to the United States from Lislevane, Timoleague, County Cork. His mother was a Sullivan from Ballyporeen, County Tipperary, where Ronald Reagan's people also came from.

Joe Murphy's parents met and married in New York and never returned to Ireland. They came by ship—there was no other way—and the journey was long and expensive. His father was a teamster for most of his life and his mother began as a cook for a Long Island family. She died when Joe Murphy was 15 and his father died when Joe was 39. "Since my father did not communicate very well, I did not identify as Irish and grew up dealing with Americans *per se*. Myself and my two sisters were raised as Americans not knowing much about our family and having no other relatives here".

After school at the Good Shepherd Grammar School, Joe Murphy first came in contact with the Irish Christian Brothers at Rice High School shortly before his mother died. "I wasn't an all-star academic", he says, "but I received a scholarship to Iona College. It was Brother Darcy, now head of the Order, who called me in one day and said 'we'd like to have you at Iona as a student'".

During the Korean War, Murphy volunteered for the Marines and then resumed college on the G.I. Bill of Rights. He graduated in 1959 as a Bachelor of Business Administration, majoring in accountancy, and spent the next seven years in public accounting at Price Waterhouse and Co. and Parnell Kerr Forster.

In 1966 he joined Laurence Wien, the owner of the Empire State Building and other major properties, in a major real estate syndication. "I sold the interests that I owned for over $1 million and that was the basis of my present personal wealth", he says. "I was 35 years old".

Murphy's first link with the Belgian group was formed in 1970 when he co-founded and became President of the Lambert Brussels Real Estate Corporation, which owns and operates about $100 million of commercial real estate in the United States. It was through this company that the merger with Drexel Burnham came about in 1976. The net cost then was $20 million; the net value now is over $200 million.

"When one grows up", reflects Joe Murphy, "one begins to ask: Where am I from? How did I get to be here?" A watershed in his life was reached when he made his first visit to Ireland 10 years ago in search of his roots. He had written to a member of the family without knowing what he wanted. "When I arrived in Ireland, nobody was there and I was not comfortable. Then in 1982 one of my first cousins wrote a long letter apologising for the silence and on the telephone I suggested a family get-together in the form of a dinner party.

"Then the most miraculous thing happened. There was a pause on the phone and my cousin said the dinner idea was nice but 'we were thinking of a reunion Mass for our deceased parents'. That was a striking concept to me in the 20th century.

"One of my other cousins was chaplain to a hospital, so we had Mass in the private chapel and then dinner. The family is still in Cork, Lislevane and Kinsale, where my ancestors were in the hotel and hospitality business. During a visit to the home of one of my cousins, whose house was built by my grandfather, I saw a large oil painting of my grandfather painted when he was in the Royal Navy. I had a moustache then and as I looked it appeared as if I was gazing into a mirror image of myself.

"Most of my relatives live in the area of Cork City, and that's where we had the reunion in 1983. There were 50 of us at table. In 1984 there were 140 and we invited an entire family that I didn't know existed in Indianapolis. My grandfather had ten brothers and sisters and after a few generations that makes for a large family. One branch of the Murphys are builders in Dublin. By next year I'll need to lease Croke Park in Dublin to house the family reunion.

"My oldest uncle—and the only one still alive—says that my father took another uncle's ticket and left for America. The ones that stayed at home all worked for a general store in Cork City, near where Jury's Hotel is now. My father and uncles all fought in the Irish Republican Army in the War of Independence and were honoured by the Irish Government and I reckon that's what America is all about. America became great because it became home to people who were unwilling to accept conditions in their native lands. They realised that there had to be a better way, migrated to the U.S. and set up a new life for themselves and their children. I can appreciate that people would rather dig holes here in New York City than remain subservient at home. These strong and brave migrants of the great American miracle".

Joe Murphy is married to Jo Ann Mazella, also of New York City, and they have five children. Joseph Junior is 25 and running two of the four hotels Joe Murphy owns. Patricia is Joe's twin and completing her master's degree at Iona College. Christopher is 23 and along with Carolyn, 22, went to Syracuse University. Patricia also attended Syracuse for her undergraduate work. Mary (19) is at Boca Roton College, Florida, a Marymount foundation lately taken over by the city. The family lives in Scarsdale, New York.

Joe Murphy attended the Graduate School of Business Administration of New York University, but his heart is still with Iona College in New Rochelle, where he is a trustee, a member of the Executive Committee and Chairman of the Finance Committee. In 1983, Iona gave him an honorary doctorate, but most important to him and the college is that the much-lauded Murphy Science and Technology Center is named after his parents and in honour of the Christian Brothers, who have had such a major positive impact on his life.

"I gave the naming gift", he says, failing to add that it was one million dollars. "I was so deeply indebted to the Christian Brothers that I want to honour them and pay tribute to the memory of my parents".

EMMETT O'CONNELL

"ABOUT 350 investors came to hear the latest news from Managing Director Mr. Emmett O'Connell, who had flown back from Colombia especially for the occasion. A charismatic figure, Mr. O'Connell did not disappoint his disciples". That is how *The Irish Times* reported the annual general meeting in Dublin of Eglinton Oil and Gas in July, 1984. After the meeting, Emmett O'Connell was pushed by shareholders for "the real story: what are the shares worth in your estimation?". His reply was short and to the point: "I am an oil man, not a stockbroker".

O'Connell, who felt "the lure of the oil" in 1977, is also a director of Osceola Hydrocarbons and of Texas Continental Securities. He is that rare species, an Irish American now living mostly in Ireland but equally at home in the two cultures. His family's familiarity with both sides of the Atlantic is exemplified by his sister Deirdre, director of the Focus Theatre in Dublin and an apostle of the Method system of training and rehearsal for actors which bases a performance on inner emotional experience, discovered largely through the medium of improvisation rather than on the teaching or transmission of technical expertise. Konstantin Stanislavsky first tried these ideas in the Moscow Arts Theatre, but they were developed in America by the director Lee Strasberg who founded the Actors' Studio in New York in 1947. That was where Deirdre O'Connell learned what she propounds today in company with Marlon Brando and Paul Newman.

Another sister of Emmett O'Connell's is Geraldine, who taught school for several years on the Seminole Indian Reservation in Florida and was chosen as one of three people to represent the 5,000 Seminole Indians at the recent quadrennial conference of Indians in Denver. The other two were genuine Indians. She is one of the two people who first devised a phonetic alphapet for the Seminoles in Florida, that unfortunate tribe which in 1836 under their leader Osceola (which is where the oil company got its name) attacked the whites in protest against their enforced removal west of the Mississippi. After bloody battles and bloodier massacres, the Seminoles held the Americans to a draw in 1842. The Americans invited Osceola to negotiate under a flag of truce, but when he appeared Osceola was seized and flung into prison, where he died.

These were some of the people of whom Christopher Columbus wrote to the King and Queen of Spain: "So tractable, so peaceable, are these people that I swear to your Majesties there is not in the world a better nation". In 1829, Andrew Jackson became President of the United States, a man known to the Seminoles, the Cherokees and the other tribes of the South as Sharp Knife, because in his frontier days he had slain them in their thousands. Jackson promised a promise that would never be broken. But it was, and the Indians were moved on again.

Emmett O'Connell was born in the Bronx, New York, in June, 1936. His father, who had him christened after Robert Emmet, the Irish patriot hanged in 1803, thought that there were two ts in Emmet, and the name stuck. He was a native of Ballisodare, County Sligo, and was an organiser with Mike Quill's Transport Workers' Union until he became a civil servant. His wife was from near Banteer, County Cork, and they had five children.

As well as Deirdre and Geraldine, there is a third sister, Gretta, who is married to Patrick Collins, an American oil company executive. Deirdre, it should be said, was married to the late Luke Kelly, a leading member of The Dubliners, probably the best known group in the world of Dublin traditional musicians and ballad singers. Geraldine now lives in Dublin and speaks fluent Irish which she learned through the Gaelic League. Emmett O'Connell's older brother Kevin, now retired from the New York Police Department, lives in Austin, Texas, where he is an active member of the Ancient Order of Hibernians.

O'Connell's first capital was amassed in California where he did contracting in the oil refineries just north of San Francisco. "I was at that for five years. We were in the mainstream of the Vietnam war and there was a construction boom in the petro-chemical industry, particularly in California.

"In 1969 I went to Ireland. My first job was as assistant company engineer in Robert Wilson and Company in Lisburn, County Antrim. This was a traditional knackers' yard where old horses were slaughtered and processed. Wilson's was upgrading its product to a chemical rendering process and had taken over three companies in the South of Ireland. I was there for a year doing mechanical engineering and plant installation.

"Simultaneously, with Uinseann MacEoin the Dublin architect, I had bought the publishing rights to *Development*, *Plan* and *Stream and Field* magazines. We set up a new company called Pomeroy Press Ltd., and in 1970 I left engineering to go full-time into publishing. I became editor of *Development*; Uinseann MacEoin became editor of *Plan*, and Finn Gallen, who is now with the Irish Industrial Development Authority in New York, became editor of *Stream and Field*.

"I edited *Development* until March, 1972, when I formed Investors Portfolio Finance Ltd., which was Dublin based. The company and I were doing exceptionally well until one day my picture appeared in the English *Sunday Times* over the caption: 'A leading member of the I.R.A.'

"The paper published an apology and a withdrawal, but I lost the majority of the large portfolios that I had been managing. The only substance to what the *Sunday Times* had alleged was that I had attended an economic conference on the concept of a federal Ireland and had written a pamphlet based on federalism and entitled 'Shaping a New Society'". During the 70s O'Connell was a prolific writer on economic and political matters. In addition to three pamphlets, he had over 100 articles published in various papers and magazines.

"I then started a company called Numismatic Metals. Apart from the four main commercial banks, mine was the only company in the Republic licensed to trade in gold". O'Connell sold out this company in 1975 but not before he reputedly had made a large fortune in English sovereigns and Krugerrands, the South African gold bullion coins first minted in 1967 "to put gold into the hands of the man in the street". In 1975, 4.8 million mass-produced Krugerrands were sold wordwide.

"I went into farming and spent a most enjoyable bucolic existence for three years. First I had cattle in Woodenbridge, County Wicklow, where I went to live. Then I moved to Foulksmills, County Wexford, where I still live and farm on 305 acres. . I have a suckling herd and I grow barley".

Then Emmett O'Connell recalls June of 1973— the month is important—when he wrote a number of articles of which he is immensely proud. They were sub-titled: "Oil, Arabs and the Next War" and they predicted that because the price of oil was abnormally low in terms of the cost of any other mineral, a crunch was inevitable. Four months later this remarkable exercise in prophecy was fulfilled, but "even when the inevitable price rise came, the accepted wisdom remained that OPEC would collapse and oil would once again be cheap, though not as cheap as it was before October, 1973.

"In 1977 I felt the lure of the oil myself, and a group of 15 private investors put up IR£260,000 to back us in trading oil-leases in the American Mid-West. This was an inexpensive way of getting into the oil game.

"We believed that oil prices would go up from $11 a barrel and in that belief we bought leases that were considered marginal at the reigning prices. Our group was depending on some local American operators whom we believed to be capable people. But we soon learned after 28 dry holes in a row that Americans can be just as incompetent as any and we became totally independent of others.

"That is why in November, 1979, we formed Eglinton Oil and Gas. Why the name Eglinton? The truth is we had a devilish tough time finding a name that had not been registered. Time was running short and in frustration I looked out the office window in Dublin and saw Eglinton Road. 'Try Eglinton Oil and Gas', I said. By such means are great corporate decisions taken.

"That original IR£260,000 was at 20p. a share. That November we raised an additional IR£260,000 at 25p. a share. Now the company is worth over IR£50 million. It is a remarkable story of successes in Texas and Oklahoma and is the first Irish company ever to explore for oil and gas in America. Five of the original investors are Irish Americans; the rest were Irish. There are now over 3,000 shareholders.

"We were also the first Irish company to go into South America, to Colombia, where we are getting encouraging results". (At the company's annual general meeting in July, 1984, the Chairman, Niall O'Connor, said the company was adequately funded to complete its exploration programme in the area of the Colombia concession currently being explored).

Emmett O'Connell says that Eglinton was given such a major contract area by the National Oil Company of Colombia in order to prod the oil majors into stepping up their own exploration programmes.

In 1981, O'Connell set up a second company in Belfast. He was the organiser and founder of Bryson Oil and Gas but he brought in David Stafford of the County Wexford shipping family as Managing Director. "The object of locating in Belfast was to get outside the recent exchange controls which made it very difficult for Irish people to invest outside the country. Also I felt that Northern Ireland had been severely neglected in the Irish oil boom and that there would be a large number of Northern Ireland investors, which proved to be true.

"Bryson joined Eglinton in the Colombia venture. Bryson is

quoted on the London Stock Exchange, where its value is put at £25 million sterling. Eglinton is also a public company quoted on both the London and Dublin exchanges.

"Then I teamed up with some Irish Americans in Texas to form Osceola Hydrocarbons, which was based in Belfast first but in May, 1984, moved to Dublin". Osceola had a very successful introduction in July, 1984, to the Dublin and London markets, with 800,000 shares placed representing 20 percent of the company's four million shares.

One financial writer for a Dublin newspaper wrote: "It takes some guts to bring a company to the market these days, when high interest rates are restraining performance generally". The Chairman of Osceola is Pádraig Ó Nualláin, former Managing Director of New Ireland Assurance Company and holder of about 20,000 shares in Osceola, which has joined Eglinton and Bryson in the Colombia consortium. Ó Nualláin is also a director of Jim Delaney's and Emmett O'Connell's Texas Continental Securities, the Dublin-based venture capital company.

O'Connell says Osceola moved its base because he feels Dublin "could and should develop its own Stock Exchange as a financial services centre capable of contributing a great deal in export earnings and direct tax revenue to the Irish economy. The estimated value of Osceola is IR£5 to IR£10 million and its field of interests includes the Gulf of Mexico, Germany, Colombia and the Mid-West. We have a host of Irish American and Northern Ireland investors", he says.

"But closest to my own heart is a group of Irish people and Irish Americans who had done rather well in oil shares and have decided to return some of the profits into Ireland by establishing what is essentially a merchant bank, though not in name because that would be to subject it to onerous regulation by the Central Bank of Ireland.

"This is Texas Continental Securities, the underlying concept of which is to provide management and financial expertise to assist small and not so small Irish companies to so structure themselves as to attract new equity investment and eventually obtain a Stock Exchange quotation.

"Texas Continental will also be used as a funnel, or broker, to introduce American equity capital into qualified Irish companies, the idea always being to provide a takeout for the new equity investors through the mechanism of the Stock Exchange quotations.

"The vast majority of Irish companies are closely-held, family-dominated companies whose shares have no public market and a limited transferability. The result is that any investment in such companies is regarded as dead money. T.C.S. will seek to change that by encouraging closed companies to accept new shareholders and thus dilute the ownership of the original management or family.

"The burden of bank borrowings will thus be lessened and new capital will be injected into Irish industry making it both highly profitable and free-market oriented. I have had a missionary zeal over this project for the last two years and the ideology that it represents goes back even further, certainly four to five years". O'Connell has always maintained that Irish investors are some of the most interested in the world. However, as he told the *Wall Street Journal* recently, they do not like to be told anything other than good news.

Emmett O'Connell met Raphael O'Kelly of Newbridge, County Kildare, at a tennis dance in Dublin. They married (she is known as Ray) and they have three children. Roisín, who is 21, is in her final year at Trinity College, Dublin, where she read Ancient Civilisations. Robert Emmet (one t in the interests of history) is 15 and going to St. Peter's College, Wexford, and the youngster is Oisín Donnchadha, who is at the local national school.

With the business side of his life dealt with, Emmett O'Connell enlarges on his historical perspective of Ireland. "One hundred years ago", he says, "the sense of being Irish was embodied in the Fenian movement, which was conspiratorial and secretive but also internationalist, with connections in Australia, Canada, France and the United States.

"With the foundation of the Irish Free State in 1922 all that changed. No longer were the Irish like the Wandering Jew. The mantle of moral authority now rested with the legitimacy of the Dublin Government. This change caused the people of the Irish diaspora to look for a lead to Dublin and this sense of searching for leadership was greatly enhanced when Éamon de Valera came to power in 1932 because he had the mystique and had been born in the United States and often came here. By his use of radio he sent greetings to the Irish abroad. Dev knew how to reach back and pluck that particular string of the harp".

O'Connell stands up. "Now what happens?", he exclaims. "There is another shift. The Government in Dublin became more isolationist and parochial until finally they became myopic. Nobody now, except perhaps Seán MacBride, has that sense of internationalism, so they belittle it in others.

"They display a meanness of attitude that portrays the only real Irish as belonging in one geographic location, the Twenty-Six Counties. This shift was brought to a head as the Government stood idly by and did nothing constructive about the North. And the Irish abroad looked on in confusion and bewilderment as the Government thus abandoned its legitimacy.

"During the hunger strike of 1981 while the world's attention was riveted on the strikers, the FitzGerald Government callously ignored them and supported the British attitude of no concessions. Suddenly the Irish abroad felt there was no longer any centre for legitimation of the wider definition of the Irish identity.

"One result of this alienation has been the renascence of the Irish abroad. Now again we see the threads of the Irish diaspora. That's the signficance of the Irish American Unity Conference and the expansion of the A.O.H. The wheel is come full circle and the connections with Irish organisations in Britain, Australia and Canada are reestablished".

JOHN KERRY O'DONNELL

THE stormy petrel of Gaelic games in New York is John "Kerry" O'Donnell, owner of Gaelic Park in the Bronx and a man who is on record as not denying that he is a millionaire. Yet in 1984, the association's centenary year, he will tell you: "The biggest mistake I made was having anything to do with the Gaelic Athletic Association".

The truth is that John Kerry O'Donnell has kept the spirit of the games alive in New York, 3,000 miles from their home, during a long and tempestuous career as "Mr. G.A.A." in the city; that he has made friends and admirers everywhere in spite of his forthrightness—"I hope their stay in Purgatory will be extended", he says of two deceased Presidents of the Association—and that in spite of his 85 years he has remained flexible in the face of radically shifting attitudes towards Gaelic games; the sudden change in the U.S. immigration laws in 1965, and the flight of the Irish from the Bronx and other neighbourhoods to the affluent suburbs fifty miles away.

His battles with the Central Council of the G.A.A. in Dublin are legendary. "I've a fierce name for fighting", he says, and recounts the story he told Dave Guiney, the famous sports writer, when Guiney asked him how his relations stood with the Central Council:

"When the men were being fed in our kitchen during the threshing, they'd have bread and butter and a bowl of milk. My mother noticed that one young fellow was not drinking his milk and she asked why. 'There's a mouse in it', he said. Quietly and quickly she fished out the mouse, threw it over the half-door and went about her business looking after the other lads. When she went back to the young fellow, he was still looking at the bowl of milk. He hadn't touched it. 'What's wrong with you?' says she. 'You don't want your milk with a mouse in it and you don't want your milk with no mouse in it'. That's the way I am with the Central Council".

That half-door through which Mrs. O'Donnell threw the mouse—and who is to say she didn't?—was in the house in Gleann na nGealt, near Camp in County Kerry, where John O'Donnell was born. (In one of the most famous sagas of the Fianna in the Third Century A.D., the King of France was so frightened out of his wits by a mighty battle against Fionn and the Fianna that he took wing for Gleann na nGealt—the Valley of the Mad People).

John Kerry, as he was nicknamed in New York later, was a very young man when he emigrated, the first of the family to leave home. "You're gone before you realise the difference", he says. "You're in a strange country with no place to go. After a little you realise how inexperienced you are and how little qualification you have to start life with. But you adjust and you move into the customs of the new country. The will to survive, I believe, is strong, stronger in the emigrant than in the native, who has it too easy.

"I first came to Montreal in Canada and by chance met cousins of whose existence I had no idea. I was sent—people recognised that I was not a native—to a Christian Brothers' school where they put me in touch with a man called O'Donnell who turned out to be from the next parish, but only the ruins of the old house he came from remained when I left home. It was through me that Bishop O'Donnell went back to his native place in Gleann na nGealt.

"I went north from Montreal to work as a lumberjack. The way the system worked was that an agent in Montreal recruited you. He got a commission, so when you weren't too long working he arranged for you to be laid off and he got another commission for recruiting your replacement.

"I went then to New York for a while and then to Detroit. There I spent four years and got involved in baseball and stuff like that while I worked for the Dodge car factory. I also went to school, to Cass High School to learn bricklaying and plan-reading.

"I returned to New York in 1926 and by then I was more Yank than Irish. But I went home in 1927 or 28 and it was only then that I got into football, in the West Kerry League. When I returned to New York I got interested in the G.A.A. here". (Kerry pioneered by making a U.S. tour in 1927. In 1931, during the famous four-in-a-row run from 1929 to 1932 when John Kerry's brother Tim was playing, Kerry returned to New York and drew 60,000 to Yankee Stadium in a game against New York).

"I was making $99 a week take home pay, a lot of money in those days. Then the Wall Street Crash and the Depression came. I remember the joke going around about the prospective tenant of a top-floor apartment. The landlord says to him: 'Is that to live in or do you want to jump?'

"People say we're loud but you'd have to be loud in those boom years because there were so many structures going up and so much ironwork and riveting going on that you had to shout or not be heard. You felt that this would never end. There were pages of jobs advertised every day in the *World*.

"After the crash I was offered a job at $12 and I thought I might as well be idle. I was out of work for three years. Patcheen Clifford the great Kerry footballer—his wife was a cousin of mine—they kept me for the three years. Otherwise I don't know what would have happened.

"You couldn't picture the hunger. There were five or six of us Kerry fellows in a rooming house down in a basement hoping someone would invite us for a cup of coffee. Somebody said there was a man down at 42nd Street and Fifth Avenue selling apples. We were living at 96th Street and Columbus Avenue. Would you believe it, we walked all the way down there just to look at the apples. We didn't have a nickel to buy one. People went to Innisfail Park not to watch the games but to find someone who would give them 10 cents. There was no admission charge after 1937.

"Then the country went to war, and nothing became plenty", he says.

In the meantime John Kerry O'Donnell began to rise in the world and by 1935 he had his first saloon bar. "Would you believe it, I could have been in the saloon business earlier but I thought I wasn't the type, that I wasn't qualified to be the happy-go-lucky man shaking hands with everybody and yessing people to death. I couldn't have been more wrong. All the people wanted was a clean place, give them their change, and allow no barflies or moochers to interfere with them".

In ten years he had four or five saloons going, and at the same time, having played football with the Kerry Club of New York in the early 1930s, he "became more of a manager" and was deeply involved with the club from 1932 to 1972.

Seven times he has been elected President of the New York G.A.A., properly known as the Gaelic Athletic Association of Greater New York, which controls New York championships in hurling and football. His first Presidency was in 1940, his second in 1955. Then in 1958 he succeeded his good friend Michael Flannery, who was Grand Marshal of the St. Patrick's Day Parade in 1983, and retained the Presidency for three years. Again in 1972 and 1973 John O'Donnell was

President, a position that was first created in 1915 when Thomas Brady of Cavan was elected. In 1984 the Presidency is held by Oliver O'Donnell.

John Kerry is quick to point out that before Jimmy Mahony, Patcheen Clifford and himself got control of the Kerry Club, Kerry had won one championship; since 1972 they have won none, "but while we were on the scene Kerry won 22. So we had something beyond the ordinary—let's put it that way without bragging. It wasn't winning that gave me pleasure so much as beating the other fellow, especially Cork".

In 1944-45 Jim Cotter, who was President of the G.A.A. in New York at the time, asked John Kerry O'Donnell and Barney Prendergast, "a great Mayoman", if they would take over Gaelic Park. Paul Russell, the Kerry footballer and a great friend of O'Donnell's, has said that the park would have been lost to the soccer people but for O'Donnell. "Cotter was a great Corkman. All Corkmen would have you believe they're great but some would have a tough time convincing me. I have periods of pity for them once in a while, but Jim was a rare individual, and when he asked me to come in with Barney I said I would because of the admiration I had for Barney. He's dead since.

"But Barney pulled out and I hadn't brains enough to do the same. The war was on, there was no one coming out from home, and things were bad. I was in Gaelic Park only a short time when I was down to one bar. The park was dragging me down. I regret going into it all the time. My wife Helen—she's American but of Kerry extraction—was exceptionally good at helping me".

The biggest event of those years was bringing the All-Ireland Final to the Polo Grounds in New York in 1947. The Very Rev. Michael Canon Hamilton from County Clare was the representative of the New York G.A.A. to the Central Council. Through his persuasion the Central Council agreed to hold the football All-Ireland between Kerry and Cavan in New York and 35,000 people came to see Cavan win. John Kerry O'Donnell, who is credited with the major part in organising such a mighty event in the annals of the G.A.A., says "the finagling with the Central Council that time was indescribable. Great men came out here and decided the grounds were too small. Then they changed their minds, as they often did. But they never changed their minds about me—they always tried to bury me".

In spite of his celebrated differences with Padraig O'Keeffe, the late secretary of the G.A.A., O'Donnell sold $136,000 worth of tickets in advance, and O'Keeffe later affirmed to Mick Dunne, the noted radio and television sports commentator, that "without John O'Donnell that All-Ireland would never have been played".

In the 1950s, New York entered the National League and won it, playing against Cavan in Croke Park before a crowd of 33,000 on July 30th, 1950. Immigration was at full flood and the G.A.A. was taking the cream of the crop into the county teams in America. Competition was at an all-time high, and through the good offices of the late Patrick J. Grimes and of John O'Donnell, the All-Ireland Finals began to be broadcast from Ireland. In Gaelic Park, charitable causes were given field days and great clergymen such as the late Cardinal Cushing spoke fondly of the G.A.A. and its great work for the Catholic Church.

"A lot of people think the G.A.A. is Catholic", says O'Donnell, "and I don't blame them for thinking that. It's about time we got a letter from a Protestant Archbishop saying he's proud to belong to the G.A.A. Sam Maguire (who donated the coveted All-Ireland football cup) was a Protestant. He was proud of what he did but you don't read the things he said. He and others, like me, didn't do it for honour and glory, but for love of the game".

In the 1950s, controversy with the Central Council reached a new height. "Individually", says O'Donnell, "they are the most intelligent people you'd find, but put them together—you can have 'em. When you're right, you can take on the best of them and scatter them.

"You ask me if I was disappointed in 1981 not to get elected in Killarney to the Presidency of the G.A.A. All I can say is that white sheep eat more than black ones because there are more of them. I know my limitations but I also know the years I put into the game. This isn't ego, but modesty can be taken too far".

The celebration of the New York G.A.A.'s golden jubilee in 1964 evoked a rare degree of unity between Dublin and New York. A spectacular series of events was staged beginning with a match in Gaelic Park between Tipperary, the 1964 National League hurling champions, and Kilkenny, 1963 All-Ireland champions, for the first World Hurling Cup ever offered (by the Ruppert Brewery of New York). The result of this clash between the historic hurling rivals was Kilkenny 4-16, Tipperary 3-13.

John Kerry O'Donnell took three months off that summer and in August the New York G.A.A. conducted the first ever Round-the-World football tour, ending with a banquet in Birr given by the Offaly County Board. Sponsored by Ballantine's Brewery to the tune of $35,000, the tour included San Francisco; Auckland, New Zealand;

Melbourne and Sydney, Australia. O'Donnell has strong views about the Australian Rules game. "The people we played were G.A.A., not Australian Rules. There's no such thing as a wedding between the oval ball and the round ball. It's like crossing a kangaroo with a descendant of the Dingle puck goat".

The golden jubilee was rounded off by the National League final played in Gaelic Park by New York and Dublin and won by the home side by 2-12 to 1-13. It was New York's second league title, a magnificent performance.

The following year saw the enactment of the U.S. Immigration Law. Few in the Irish community could have foreseen its effect: anyone who did must have remained silent as the law went through Congress under the guidance of an Irish American Attorney-General, Robert F. Kennedy. The law did away with the traditional ethnic quota system and limited immigration to those with professions and trades for which there was a need in the United States.

In 1968 the Round-the-World tour was repeated. Both tours were made in the name of Cardinal Cushing, Archbishop of New York, who later was instrumental in having John Kerry made a Knight Commander of the Order of St. Gregory, a papal honour of which he is so proud that he has been known to wear the full regalia to the Bank of Ireland All Stars Banquet in Dublin.

"Those Cardinal Cushing tours", he says, "were never equalled by teams from Ireland: copied, but never equalled. You're talking to the trail-blazer. Some of the players still remember the tour as the biggest thrill of their lives—just to be a Cardinal Cushing player, hurling or football".

The great achievement of those games, which ended in 1973, was that players from the weakest counties such as Leitrim and Westmeath got a chance to take part. Indeed, as John O'Donnell will tell you, "that was the whole idea".

As the Cushing games ended, things looked black for Gaelic games and Gaelic Park. But O'Donnell wasn't finished yet. A South Pacific Hurling Tour under John O'Donnell and Mick Morrissey (President of the New York G.A.A. in 1975 and 1976) was a huge success in 1973 and in 1974 John Kerry announced that the Carrolls All Stars (in 1979 taken over by the Bank of Ireland) and the 1974 All Ireland hurling and football champions would play in New York in April, 1975. The Gaelic games scene was transformed; the matches were a sell-out, and the G.A.A.'s International Fund was on its way back into the black.

But the visits of the Bank of Ireland G.A.A. All Stars are not going to save the life of Gaelic games in New York. It is in the minor movement which began in 1969 that the future lies. The movement, which got a great fillip in 1972 when the Good Shepherd Minor Football Club from the Inwood section of Manhattan made the first Irish tour by a U.S. -born minor team, has been very successful, due in no small measure to Bill Burke of the Bank of Ireland, who was President of the Minor Board a few years ago.

Some of the young people do not even have Irish blood. "In a sense", says John Kerry, "the American playing Gaelic football is playing a foreign game". By using that phrase he is looking back to the famous or notorious G.A.A. ban on foreign games in Ireland. "The minors have to be the hope of the future—provided they have a junior championship to aspire to when they get older.

"No, it doesn't occur to me to be saddened by the scarcity of people attending the games at Gaelic Park compared with the heyday of G.A.A. here. Pride takes the place of sorrow".

Talking about his recent bout of ill-health, John Kerry O'Donnell says: "Like everything else I do, when I start coming apart I make a good job of that too. But I have learnt that there's only one way to go—with your shoes on. And since I was born in 1899, I have this hope that I will have lived in three centuries".

Paul O'Dwyer

WHEREVER subway lines have been built in New York, the result has been the mass movement of people from the lower economic strata. The good people of Staten Island are quite content with the ferry to Manhattan and would quite strenuously resist the construction of a subway. That is why, when Paul O'Dwyer was running for President of the City Council in 1973, he addressed a group of Staten Island voters in these terms:

"Staten Island has never been overly kind to me. I have tried to please. It hasn't worked. I have told jokes. I have lavished praise on the Island's babies. I have remarked on the machismo of your men and the beauty, charm and grace of your women. I have avoided the issues lest the memory of my past positions arouse your anger. Nothing has helped. Now, I can tell you, if I win but don't carry Staten Island, I will run two subways here, one from Manhattan and one from Brooklyn".

His threat raised a laugh. He won the election, but without the Staten Island vote. "But at least I established that the Islanders do have a sense of humour", he says.

That says a lot about Paul O'Dwyer. As Carroll O'Connor, the well-know actor and friend of O'Dwyer's, has put it: "How do you obtain high office in New York if you insist on fighting out in the open for things like peace and constitutional rights, if you seize every opportunity to stand shoulder to shoulder with the Irish and the Jews and the Blacks and the Puerto Ricans, and even now and then with some lonely radical in danger of being stomped to death by orthodoxy?...But if you're Paul O'Dwyer, you never lose heart".

At 77 O'Dwyer shows no sign of retiring either from his law practice—O'Dwyer and Berstien— or from the relentless pursuit of justice whenever it seems to be endangered. And the New York pot calls the Dublin kettle black in an admiring reference to another fighter for human rights and champion of the underdog: "I just don't know how Seán MacBridge keeps it up. In my book, MacBride measures up as good as any. My only regret is that Ireland didn't make him President".

Tom Paine—*Common Sense* lies on O'Dwyer's desk—was a seminal influence. It is easy to see why the 18th-century Englishman appeals to this 20th-century Irish American. Paine was the son of a small farmer in Thetford, Norfolk. He became an excise officer in 1761 but was dismissed the service for agitating for the removal of grievances. His writings on the rights of the worker were brought to the attention of Benjamin Franklin who brought him to the colonies. He went to America and in 1776 published *Common Sense*, a discussion of the causes of the war with England. O'Dwyer believes that Paine's contribution had a significant effect on the Revolution. "There was severe irritation in the Colony against England", he says, "but not enough to cause the rupture. Paine's pamphlet showed why monarchy was not the way".

Paine went back to England in 1787, and in 1790, in reply to Edmund Burke's *Reflections on the French Revolution*, he published the first part of *The Rights of Man*, a forcible enunciation of the human condition which compelled him, when he wrote the second part two years later, to flee to France to avoid prosecution. There he was at once elected a member of the Convention and, forthright as ever, used his position to oppose the execution of Louis XVI. For that he was imprisoned until Robespierre died. He used the time in jail to write *The Age of Reason*, and died in America. William Cobbett, the political pamphleteer, had his body taken back to England.

Paul O'Dwyer published his often prickly autobiography, *Counsel for the Defense*, in 1979. In it, he spares neither himself nor those, including his brother Bill, who did not justify the public honours that were heaped on them. The causes he has championed, the people he has defended, the injustices he has illuminated, are as varied as the strands in American society.

Those accused of Communist Party membership in the 1930s (at a divisional meeting of the Ancient Order of Hibernians in Brooklyn, O'Dwyer's was one of only two hands raised against a motion condemning the Transport Workers' leader, Mike Quill, for being a Communist); those in organisations like Irgun Zvai Leumi and the Haganah dedicated to an independent Zionist State in Palestine ("our purpose was to get arms and ammunition and skilled manpower to Palestine so that the Irgun could conduct the fight against Britain"); those artists who fell foul of the House Un-American Activities Committee in the 1950s (Lillian Hellman, "one of my most prestigious clients", wrote in response to her subpoena: "I cannot and will not cut my conscience to fit this year's fashions . . "); those Jews, Blacks and Puerto Ricans who could not register as voters in 19 of the States because of the literacy laws; those who sought to end American involvement in Vietnam, especially Senator Eugene McCarthy with his "quiet sanity"; the Harrisburg Seven, who included Father Philip Berrigan—all these and many others were the beneficiaries of Paul O'Dwyer's selfless dedication, brilliant advocacy and hard work in the face of enormous odds.

Under all this devotion to justice lay the matrix of Ireland, the ideal of the Republic which formed the leitmotiv of O'Dwyer's life. The case of the Fort Worth Five was no different. Irish Northern Aid, which had collected £1 million in a single year, had been subjected to various Government pressures and O'Dwyer had been "keeping the agents at bay" by using the courtroom tactics for which he has become famous.

In June, 1972, after the Berrigan trial had ended in triumph for the defendants, five New York residents were brought before a federal grand jury in Fort Worth, Texas. No charge had been brought but they were rumoured to have been involved in the purchase of guns in Mexico for use in Northern Ireland. O'Dwyer and Bernstien had never charged a fee in a civil rights case and they were not about to begin now.

When the alternatives were put to the five by O'Dwyer, they opted for accepting immunity from prosecution in return for their testimony, refusing to answer questions and being imprisoned for contempt of court. "If you co-operate, you will be set free", said the judge. "You have the key to the jail in your pocket". No appeal worked and the five were imprisioned on and off until August, 1973, when Justice William O. Douglas of the Supreme Court released them. "The bail fund, raised overnight in New York saloons, was over-subscribed", says O'Dwyer.

Paul O'Dwyer was 21 before he had his first drink—and it was not in a saloon but in the house of an aunt and uncle in Chicago who made their own beer. "After that first drink it was easy", he says. He took to dropping in on Tommy Ayres who had a speakeasy at 39th Street and Third Avenue in New York, popular with people from CBS. He was conscious that whiskey was regarded as the curse of the Irish and at first he kept to beer. Then he tried cocktails, went through an Italian wine phase and then started on Jamaica rum. "Even though I avoided whiskey, I began to recognise some signs that did not please me, that were indeed a bit frightening. After a couple of false starts, I gave up drinking entirely in 1959".

Another Catholic Irish American who talked to the present writer about alcohol in 1965 was James A. "Big Jim" Farley, who had been Postmaster-General under President Roosevelt and was chairman of the Democratic Party when Paul O'Dwyer became politically active. His mother kept a bar after his father died but it was a constant source of worry to her. "She hated to think that her children were being brought up in the atmosphere of liquor. She was poor and had seen a lot of wretchedness caused by men's addiction to strong drink.

"Mother never lost a chance to advise me against the use of liquor. When I was confirmed at the age of 12, I took a pledge to abstain from alcohol until I was 21, the usual pledge given to Catholic youths. By the time I was 21, I was deep in local politics and she continued to warn me about liquor. As a result, I never started drinking and never felt the lack of it".

Unlike Jim Farley, whose people on both sides emigrated during the Famine in the 1840s, Paul O'Dwyer was born in Lismirrane, Bohola, County Mayo, in 1907. It was an event, he says, "not regarded as a blessing in my family because I was the eleventh and last in an already over-crowded five-roomed house".

His mother was a McNicholas in a village of McNicholas's, and his grandfather Pat, known as Pat-Peggy to distinguish him, had a shop that sold everything from paraffin oil to Christmas oranges. Pat-Peggy's daughter Bridget was an assistant school teacher in a nearby school when Patrick O'Dwyer was appointed teacher in the new school in Lismirrane. He was from Tullylease, County Cork, and he married Bridget and built a three-roomed cabin with a thatched roof to which a two-storey slated addition was later made.

Patrick O'Dwyer with a few others worked secretly to organise a branch of the Irish National Teachers' Organisation and before the Great War of 1914 had won some security of tenure for teachers who up to then had been hired and fired at the whim of the school manager, usually the parish priest. "The master", as he was called, acted as private tutor outside school hours; surveyor of fields for farmers who rented land from each other; bookkeeper for local shopkeepers, writer of agreements such as marriage contracts, and reader aloud of the *Freeman's Journal* or the *Irish Independent*—more than half the village was unable to read English. The Easter Rising of 1916 and the War of Independence after it meant that the papers had much news of import to impart to a concerned people.

The children were expected to work without pay. "I don't remember really liking field work; I don't remember resenting it either", says O'Dwyer. They had little privacy, no indoor plumbing and very little money.

William was the eldest and the first to leave home. He spent two years at the Irish College of Salamanca in Spain before he decided the priesthood was not for him and he went to America without telling the family, where his name was not mentioned for years.

"I don't believe that my father's attitude would have been different if he had known that one day Bill would be mayor of a town bigger than London, an ambassador equal in importance to the emissary to the Court of St. James, chairman of the Allied Control Commission governing Italy, and a General in the Army, the equal of British General Wilson, whose father had sacked Cork City. Happily, about six months before his death in 1920, my father received a conciliatory letter from Bill, and some of the atmosphere of resentment lifted".

When Paul O'Dwyer's sister May left the old home after it had stood for 70 years, he had it torn down and replaced by the O'Dwyer Cheshire Home for 30 handicapped patients. It is one of 160 such homes around the world and is part of the Cheshire Trust set up by Group Captain Leonard Cheshire of the British Air Force who was an observer of Hiroshima and Nagasaki.

By the time O'Dwyer went to the United States in 1925, four of his brothers were already there. He had been to St. Nathy's College in Ballaghaderreen—"I think my mother prevailed on the President of the college to take me in for £30 a year"—and undersized and under weight, he was no athlete. Indeed he was in America before he realised his present height of 5 feet 7½ inches. Supported by his two teacher sisters in Bohola, he had gone to University College, Dublin, but was not happy there. "Going to Dublin was a mistake", he says, and he welcomed a letter from his brother Frank in New York suggesting that he could go there, work by day and study law by night. As the neighbours left the "American wake", they pressed a coin into his hand, a total of seven dollars representing a huge gesture of generosity from the poor.

His brother had told him that steerage passengers on the Cunard White Star liner from Cobh were obliged to be deloused and have their hair cut before embarking. "If you slip the barber a shilling", Frank wrote, "you will get a neat trim. But if you fail to do so, you will arrive here bald". As it happened, he travelled second class and avoided the humiliation.

Arriving in New York he had $25 in his pocket and the suit he was wearing. His brother Frank took him to Mrs. Maguire's boarding house at 103rd Street and Columbus Avenue, where he and Jack were living.

Frank was a truck loader in Washington Market; Jack was a checker on the waterfront. Jimmy by then was a fireman and Bill had just graduated from law school. Both were married. When Bill arrived for the welcome at Mrs. Maguire's, he was a stranger with a loud voice and gold teeth who had left home before Paul O'Dwyer was born.

Several jobs and six months on, O'Dwyer enrolled as a pre-law night student at Fordham University. By day he worked at the Susquehanna Silk Mills at 32nd Street and Madison Avenue, packing bales in the shipping department. He joined the Mayomen's Association in time for a row. John O'Connor of Kerry, the grandfather of Carroll O'Connor, was the owner, editor and publisher of the *Irish Advocate* and he wanted his daughters to be allowed to ride on horseback in the St. Patrick's Day Parade. The chairman, who had held the post for 40 years, rejected the request, was defeated in the debate and said: "I can see by now this move is well organised, and I bow to the inevitable". (Pause) "I will entertain a motion that on St. Patrick's Day, on Fifth Avenue, the ladies will be mounted".

Jimmy O'Dwyer was killed in an accident on Paul O'Dwyer's nineteenth birthday, June 19, 1926, and three months later his daughter was born. It was a traumatic time for the whole family. In September O'Dwyer enrolled in the Law School of St. John's University, Queens, a Vincentian foundation designed to cater for the children of people in the lower economic bracket. (St. John's is now the repository of all of O'Dwyer's papers covering 50 years of his part in the struggle for Irish freedom from England).

His brother Bill helped him to get a better job as a checker on the waterfront and he joined the International Longshoremen's Association. About the same time he dipped a tentative toe into Democratic politics by joining the all-Jewish Kings County Young Democratic Club. "We had all", he says, "heard the story about the ward heeler who told his boss that O'Brien had become a Republican. 'That's a damned lie', said the boss. 'I saw him at Mass last Sunday'".

Summer holidays from law school were spent at sea and jumping freight cars across America and he graduated just as the Depression began. He was admitted to the Bar in 1931, but there was not work and he managed to go to sea again under Captain Michael Brennan from Carrigaholt, Co. Clare, who had for several years skippered Admiral Byrd's sailing vessel to the South Pole. They shipped out for Rio, Santos, Montevideo and Buenos Aires.

Bill O'Dwyer came up with the idea that the Mayo football team, which had just won the provincial championship, should come to New York and play a local team. He used Frank's savings, $6,500, and asked Paul O'Dwyer to make the arrangements in Ireland. Their sister, Mary Rose, was married to Bernard Durkan, captain of the Mayo team, and both were school-teachers. The ship took seven days and the train from Cobh took forever, but all the neighbours came and sat around the fire and talked. "It was good manners for one who had seen a large piece of the world to keep quiet about it", he says.

The sponsorship scheme turned out to be a financial disaster and Frank's money was lost. But the political news at home seemed not to be all bad. De Valera and the Fianna Fáil Party were awaiting their turn at office and back in New York O'Dwyer said to the veteran I.R.A. man Connie Neenan: "I suppose, Connie, that when de Valera gets in he will continue the fight for total freedom". "You've grown older, Paul", he said, "but you still haven't grown up. The fight is over for you and me, and if Kathleen ní Houlihan isn't dead, she's badly wounded". Six months later, Fianna Fáil was in power and not long afterwards the Military Tribunal was in use again, at first against the fascist Blueshirts but soon against the I.R.A. which was defending the Left and was soon identifying de Valera with his predecessor, W.T. Cosgrave. "After 1932", says Paul O'Dwyer in a masterpiece of understatement, "my enthusiasm for Dev dwindled".

Soon O'Dwyer found himself in the middle of the labour union movement which had been revitalised by Roosevelt's new legislation. He was defending pickets against labour-organising injunctions and opposing deportation orders against foreign-born agitators. His brother Bill, by now a magistrate, was hearing the agitators' cases. "He had the gift of discharging the pickets without antagonising the police . . . . . We never worked together better".

They had not worked well together before. Paul O'Dwyer had joined Bill in the firm of Holmes and Bernstien, but could not shake off the kid brother role. So he borrowed $300 from Bill and set up on his own at 521 Fifth Avenue "in the middle of the world", as he aptly puts it. After Bill became a magistrate, Paul moved back to his office and Oscar Bernstien became his mentor, his home a salon for actors, labour leaders, thinkers, writers, activists and politicians. His Yiddish was fluent, his respect for the Sabbath was absolute, and his determination to break out of the ghetto of peddling, tailoring or running a candy store was equalled only by his concern for individual freedom.

And Bill O'Dwyer contributed to his young brother's liberal

education by challenging some of his "more parochial and self-serving views". He said that as time went on Paul would find out things about the Irish that he did not like and many things about other Americans that he did like.

At 26, Paul O'Dwyer was accepted as a full partner into what became Holmes, Bernstien and O'Dwyer, and two years later he married Kathleen Rohan, a girl of Galway extraction. They had four children, William, Eileen, Brian and Rory. "That they grew up whole and sound I owe largely to Kathleen", he says. When she died in 1981, they were living on a farm 60 miles from New York, "very like Mayo in its vegetation and topography and stocked with Connemara ponies". He lives there still at weekends, lonely but full of compassion for the state of Ireland, which he visits once or twice a year, sometimes working with Seán MacBride on an extradition case.

O'Dwyer's readiness to represent politically difficult and diverse clients is nowhere better shown than in his present work for the Iranian Government in their quest for the Shah's money. "I took no test of popularity", he says. Oscar Bernstien died at 89 soon after O'Dwyer's inauguration as President of the City Countil of New York in 1973 and during O'Dwyer's term of office the firm of O'Dwyer and Bernstien was held together by two nephews, a son-in-law and his son Brian. Retired from politics in 1977, he returned to his Wall Street Office to take up the cudgels on behalf of his clientele of stage people, writers like Jimmy Breslin and Pete Hamill, artists and political activists of all kinds.

He is President of the Irish Institute, which has made grants to Seán MacBride's Irish Section of Amnesty International; the Yeats Summer School in County Sligo; the Library of Trinity College, Dublin; the Kilkenny Design Workshops; Ciste Colmcille, which disburses money to artists and writers; the Merriman Summer School in County Clare, and restoration of Ballintubber Abbey in County Mayo. "You could say that we blazed the way for the Ireland Fund", he says.

"Eoin McKiernan, the President of the Irish American Cultural Institute, is a very fine man, one of the noblest. One man's genius has gone into his magazine *Éire-Ireland*, and one side effect of his work is the deep interest of Irish Americans in finding out who they are.

"A lot of new organisations have grown up in the last 12 years but they don't represent the diverse positions there are. The county associations are dying out and that is natural since they were a function of 'No Irish Need Apply'. The Friendly Sons of St. Patrick is part of the Irish American sub-culture and the Ancient Order of Hibernians, which was always docile and much more Catholic than Irish, is now extremely militant.

"The membership of Irish National Caucus and Noraid are practically interchangeable. The death of the hunger strikers in 1981 gave the Northern question a new dimension. The spectacle of a young man dying as a poet took the whole thing out of the terrorist propaganda area. The Ad Hoc Committee of Congress was formed because the Four Horsemen of the Apocalypse—Kennedy, O'Neill, Carey and Moynihan—were doing nothing. They were too influenced by the Irish Government. Mario Biaggi is very popular in Irish America.

"As a reaction to the Ad Hoc Committee, the Friends of Ireland group was formed in Congress. We're really blessed because of Britain's mistakes, and now we have a Government in Ireland making one mistake after another and learning nothing. The arrogance of diplomatic office in Ireland, the U.S. and Britain has succeeded in making 'Republican' a bad word. I would be more tolerant of Charles Haughey, who has not yet had a chance to be secure in office.

"I was told several years ago that I should not have interfered politically in Irish affairs when I could have done more good by helping the Irish economy. You might have an argument against me if you were doing anything yourselves.

"Although 70 per cent of the U.K. people want the Brits out of Northern Ireland, all I can observe in Ireland is lethargy. I don't find people in the street as they were after Bloody Sunday. Government propaganda may have convinced them that taxes and the non-affordability of the North by the South are more important. The South of Ireland has been tarnished. I don't buy the propaganda that it would be injurious to have a United Ireland.

"This doesn't mean that I'm opposed to the Report of the New Ireland Forum. Those of us who have lived under Lloyd George and Asquith are probably more cautious about lighting bonfires or throwing hats in the air. I think the Forum would be well advised to continue their activities with those who were excluded from their deliberations—the paramilitaries and the Unionist politicians.

"These are forces that in any disruptive society cannot be ignored. I may tell you that any time I've been to the North I've never failed to meet and discuss with Protestant leaders. There is a lot of political maturity in guys like Andy Tyrie of the U.D.A. when I sit and talk with him.

"Communication and understanding are essential to an ultimate peaceful solution". When it is suggested to Paul O'Dwyer that the last statement could have been made by the Irish Government, the response is a blank stare.

The end of this story is set in the parish hall in Bohola where it all began. The scene is the victory celebration for Paul O'Dwyer in the contest for President of the City Council. In the chair is Father Martin McManus, who introduces O'Dwyer with these words: "On behalf of this parish, I want to welcome back a neighbour who has been greatly honoured in his adopted country. I want first to say how grateful we are to New York. It has been a haven for us when circumstances bade us go. Of course we are happy when one of our people meets with success at home or abroad, but his is a special case, and I am not here merely to praise a man who has been elected to high office but rather to pay respects to one who in his life saw injustice to his fellow citizens, to the exploited members of the Negro race, and who took up their cause . . . . The ill treatment meted out to them through the centuries is reminiscent of our own history. Regretfully, in America not all our people remember that, but our guest did. I hope New York honoured him for the right reason, and if it didn't we in this insignificant community do . . . . "

Paul O'Dwyer, remembering that night the antagonism of the parish priest of earlier years towards his family, says: "A bit of warmth and compassion had taken the place of hate and greed. At last liberation had come to Bohola".

ANTHONY J. F. O'REILLY

QUITE the most remarkable man to have come out of Ireland in a generation, Dr. Anthony J. F. O'Reilly has put his unique stamp of leadership, flair and style on so many vast enterprises on both sides of the Atlantic that it is easy to ignore the wry observer of life who lives inside. Yet to meet him is to come face to face with a refreshing candour and a penetrating humour that leave one buoyed up with his effervescence for the rest of the day.

Dr. Tony O'Reilly, described in *The Pittsburgh Press* recently as "the quintessential Irishman, affable, amusing and blessed with the gift of the gab," is all that and more. He invites envy for his charm and excites admiration for his feats. It would be wrong to set him down as a spinner of aphorisms and teller of tales; yet his love affair with words is palpable and the flavour of the man lies in the quick utterance of the unexpected response, often ironic and always very funny.

He is a big man, which helps. His height of six feet three inches is matched by a solid frame weighing 200-plus pounds. At 48 years old—he was born on May 7th, 1936—he could say that he has conquered the world of business in America and Ireland, yet he contents himself with looking back to the days in Bord Bainne, the Irish Dairy Board, when all he had was his reputation, and the launching of Kerrygold butter could have gone very sour. "My time in agriculture was the most exciting period of my life," he says. "I never had so much fun."

But first, who is Tony O'Reilly? He has been President and Chief Executive of H. J. Heinz, the fourth largest food company in America, since 1979. "Still in its infancy," he says of Heinz, pointing out that 88% of the world's people are in areas where Heinz does not sell. Undisputed leaders in tuna fish, so far ahead in frozen french fries that "I think the next market share after us is 2% and we have 56%," Heinz traditionally has concentrated on the U.S., Canadian, U.K., Australian, Italian, French and German markets, but now is looking outward to Africa, where they have made a $30 million dollar investment in Zimbabwe margarine and cooking oil, and to Japan. Altogether, Heinz products are made in 25 countries.

Domestically he says: "Nutrition is the name of the game for food companies. That's where the niches of profitability are, and though I don't think it's our job to be moralistic and necessarily to do good for the community, nutrition as it happens is an area where there is an easy companionship between good and profitability." In 1978 Heinz under O'Reilly bought Weight Watchers International which he said "essentially gives us a second label."

He is Chairman of Independent Newspapers, Ireland's largest and by far the most profitable publishing group, putting out about three million newspapers a week. O'Reilly has a 30% stake worth £8 million now: he paid £1 million for it. And while there is no parallel between O'Reilly and William Randolph Hearst or Rupert Murdoch, he is indisputably a press baron with all the political and economic influence that go with his power.

In terms of Ireland's political parties, his support buttresses Fine Gael, the dominant partner in the ruling Coalition Government, but it is important to recall that in 1969 the then Taoiseach or Prime Minister, Jack Lynch, offered O'Reilly the post of Minister for Agriculture in the Fianna Fáil Government of the time. The truth is that Tony O'Reilly, politically speaking, is a sleeping giant who has not yet even yawned.

He is Chairman of Atlantic Resources, the oil enterprise that emerged from the recovery of Fitzwilton to become a cash-rich company. Atlantic picked Union Oil and Gulf Oil as partners in the exploration of its six Celtic Sea blocks—"Gulf is in Pittsburgh and that's my city"—and Don Sheridan joined the company from Marathon.

On a Friday evening in July, 1983, O'Reilly was walking in the door of Castlemartin, his County Kildare country house, when he heard that "we had just struck Ireland's first oil discovery." In six weeks Atlantic's worth multiplied 15 fold, fortunes were made and lost and the shares seesawed as rumours and reports proliferated. O'Reilly regrets "the short-term focus of attention on Atlantic, which should be seen in the round over five years. The geology is subtle and complex and oil and gas discovery is a ratio game."

He reminds you that after the find he said: "You have to remember that up until a few months ago Ireland was one of the most postponable events in the world of hydrocarbons. I believe that this will be shown to be the most important event in Ireland's limited exploration history. It's Europe's last potential oil province and in the next ten years we'll hear a lot more about the Celtic Sea."

He is Chairman of Fitzwilton, a holding company that developed from Fitzwilliam Securities, formed in 1971 by O'Reilly, Vincent

Ferguson, Nicholas Leonard and Sean McKone, a childhood friend. The largest part of the conglomerate, which included textiles and zinc ore exploration, was born of an accident, the tragic air accident that killed the cream of Ireland's entrepreneurial talent in 1972. Con Smith's Ardagh Holdings was taking over W. and H. M. Goulding the fertiliser company when he died.

"I knew Gouldings was going well and I was in West Virginia a day or so after the crash when (Sir) Basil Goulding telephoned to ask me whether our two companies might merge. That was the genesis of Fitzwilton."

When the fertiliser business collapsed in 1975-76 "in the most unbelievable chaos since 1960," Fitzwilton with Moroccan rock phosphate going from $14 to $66 went through a traumatic period, gradually shedding activities to become the asset-rich vehicle that backed Atlantic Resources. But in the process Gouldings, pared of its fat from 850 employees down to 88, made £1.5 million in 1984, producing the same tonnage.

He is Chairman of the Ireland Fund, set up in 1976 on the model of the American United Jewish Appeal with a list of directors that reads like a Who's Who in Irish America. Under the banner of "Culture, Peace, Charity," the Ireland Fund distributes grants to deserving Irish organisations throughout the 32 Counties as a counterbalance to the Irish American money that is collected for Irish Northern Aid.

"The directors know what the Irish problem is," says O'Reilly. "They know it is complex and difficult, but it is well chronicled in the Report of the New Ireland Forum which we will disseminate to Irish Americans who, for many reasons, have eschewed contact with Irish American organisations.

"As well as allocating funds, we act as an information and discussion centre for the policies of reconciliation." The members are composed of Orange and Green, with the Westons and the Eatons co-operating with the Rooneys and the Dunfeys.

"There are no simple solutions to the Northern Ireland problem," O'Reilly stresses, "but assuming there were to be a community answer, America would be the great underwriter for it. Ireland would need a Marshall Plan, endorsed by the Senate and the House. Public opinion must be mobilised as the Jews have unambiguously done. The United Jewish Appeal sent $450 million to Israel last year under the aegis of a coalition of understanding; but more important than that, they caused Congress to give well over $2 billion.

"Burntollet was Ireland's Selma, where the Northern Ireland civil rights marchers were set upon by the reactionaries. It was the lowest point of British politics, Catholic Blacks versus Protestant Whites—a civil rights campaign fought and in my view largely won through the television camera."

Speaking to M. McDevitt Rubin of *The Pittsburgh Press* in March, 1984, Dr. O'Reilly said: "My own view is that the most my generation can hope for is a federal solution..... if there's going to be any change for the moment it will certainly not be a unitary state..." On another platform he said: "In order to unite Ireland, we have to stop using history as a signpost to the future."

Of the Republic as it stands, O'Reilly despairs. "Whatever the grotesqueries of the Lemass era in Ireland, the country was not paralysed as it is now. What breaks a deadly gavotte like that, I don't know. There is a Celtic genius for self-destruction that means the politicians are functioning at the margin. On the democratic menu, the buying of votes is inherent in the proportional representation system."

From the 1960s, when Seán Lemass was Taoiseach, the conferring of honorary doctorates on distinguished public servants or businessmen became commonplace and thus debased. It is good therefore to learn that Tony O'Reilly's doctorate was earned the hard way through writing a Ph. D. thesis on agricultural marketing for the University of Bradford, England, "a labour of love that began in 1970 and took me ten years." Of course he is not short of honorary doctorates either.

Born on Dublin's North Side, Anthony J. F. O'Reilly is the son of John P. O'Reilly, a barrister and civil servant from Drogheda, County Louth, and Aileen O'Connor O'Reilly of Athlone, County Westmeath, an enormously important influence on his life. "The last five yards to the line were hers," he says. "She gave me the will to win and a sense of humour." She is 70 this year.

An only child—"I got all the focus and attention and affection that normally has to be shared with four or five others"—he credits his father with being both parent and pal, "the best combination of both. I'd like to replicate the relationship." Of all his son's achievements, his father, who died in 1976, was most pleased when he acquired control of the *Drogheda Independent* as part of the Independent Newspapers group.

The Jesuits in Belvedere College, Dublin, taught him, and it was there that the love of rugby football began. "O'Reilly's career," says a contemporary, "could have been taken from the pages of Ripley's Believe It or Not. Even his selection on the Irish rugby team after only a handful of club games contains fairytale qualities. Three mediocre games and one blinder for Ireland and at the age of 19 he is picked for the Lions Tour." For the record, O'Reilly played for Ireland 29 times and for the British Lions team ten times. He was a member of the Lions Tour of South Africa in 1955 and of the Tour of New Zealand and Australia in 1959. He was the top try-scorer on both tours, creating a record that still stands.

Asked what his business philosophy is, he once replied: "In rugby, I would infuriate the crowd by laying low, inspecting the field and only attempting a long-run shot at the goal if I thought there was a reasonable chance of success. I'm the same in business as in rugby."

At University College, Dublin, he became an honours graduate in civil law and, at 22, a solicitor. He took courses in finance at the Dublin summer session of the Wharton School of the University of Pennsylvania. Jobs were scarce in Ireland so he went to work with an industrial consultancy in the North of England and then with Suttons of Cork, a firm of merchants specialising in agricultural products.

Because of his fame as a rugby player, his public profile was higher than most, but it was still a major surprise when at the age of 25 he was appointed managing director of Bord Bainne, the Irish Dairy Board. The surprise was universal—even O'Reilly had not heard of Bord Bainne when he was headhunted for the job. He was a spectacular success—"a motion calling for my resignation was tabled at almost every board meeting by the milk manufacturers, but it was the ordinary milk producers (then four major dairy co-operatives) that had the power."

Kerrygold, the brand name that he devised for Irish butter, was a major marketing achievement and created genuine added value for the farmer, but "plundering the public purse"—a favourite phrase—was a much more profitable way of adding to the farmer's wealth. One of his older colleagues, Paddy Power, said one day to O'Reilly: "Young man, I'll tell you one thing. If you're going into the Irish co-operative movement you should know that you'll get f——all co-operation from them."

One board member, highly intelligent and vituperative, told the young managing director his views about marketing Kerrygold: "Well, they have taken the decision which I think will probably ensure that your career ends in flames. I want to tell you, boys," he told the board, "you by this decision today arraign the Irish farmer face to face with the British housewife and they are patently unsuited for one another!"

"Oh Jesus," O'Reilly said to himself, "will I be able to pay the mortgage at the end of the month?"

The next move Tony O'Reilly made was reluctantly to accept the managing directorship of the Irish Sugar Company whose Erin Foods division was in deep trouble. A commanding figure in Irish public life, Lieutenant-General Michael J. Costello, had been in charge of Irish Sugar for 20 years and there has always been a clash of loyalties over the reasons for the General's departure. It was the old Humpty Dumpty question: Did he fall or was he pushed?

O'Reilly's estimate of "Micky Joe" Costello is in the circumstances generous: "Costello was an epic figure with a vision of Ireland that was both moving and worthy. The difficulty was that his idealism was not matched by a parallel ambition to be the low-cost producer. The company was simply underfinanced and burdened by a Holy Rosary of factories. I empathise, not sympathise with the General's position, which is exemplified by the fact that the company had 26,000 beet growers in Ireland whereas here in the United States there are altogether only 400 tomato growers supplying 750,000 tons a year to the H. J. Heinz Company."

In the job, which he took in December, 1966, O'Reilly's response to Erin Foods' negative sales, huge losses, large sales force and lack of products to sell was to link up with Heinz in Britain, form Heinz Erin, cut costs drastically, and create another O'Reilly winner.

Within two years, and just at the time when Jack Lynch asked him to join the Cabinet as Minister for Agriculture, Burt Gookin, chief executive officer of the parent H. J. Heinz in Pittsburgh and the man O'Reilly eventually replaced, invited the 32-year-old Irishman to head up Heinz U.K. Although flattered by Lynch's offer, he settled for the economic independence he would not have had in politics.

By November, 1971, he had been made Senior Vice President North America and Pacific, President and Chief Operating Officer in July, 1973, and after a meteoric rise he replaced Gookin in July, 1979. Earlier, in an interview with *Business Weekly*, he talked about Gookin: "Burt had phenomenal farm boy habits. He used to get up at five in the morning and be in work at seven. So I decided I would get in at ten to seven. Gookin would put his head around my door and say good morning, and I'd say good morning Burt .... I would then sleep until nine o'clock."

With all the targets he set himself at Heinz attained, the marriage of O'Reilly and Heinz seems set fair for years ahead. The standing of

Fitzwilton, on the other hand, depends on the success of Atlantic Resources. He has a lot of money riding on that one, and the land of O'Reilly's birth watches with vested interest as the tale unfolds.

Tony O'Reilly is married to the former Susan Cameron, an Australian from Sydney. They have three sons and three daughters. The eldest, Susan, is at Yale. Cameron (20) is at Oxford reading politics and economics. Justine (19), who was head girl at Cobham Hall in England, is at Brown. The triplets are 17, the two boys at Clongowes Wood College in County Kildare and the girl at Cobham. "They all," says O'Reilly, "feel themselves essentially Irish. I make a real effort to see them in August in Ireland and at Easter. Incidentally, I must pay homage to the Jesuits of Clongowes, though for a Belvederean to say that gives me real pain."

The Irishness of his children raises the question of what he is or feels himself to be. "I am an Irish citizen, which means that I am a resident alien of the United States. To me the term 'resident alien' sounds like oxymoron, a figure of speech in which contradictory ideas or terms are combined, like 'the House Ethics Committee,' 'the Carter Administration' or 'the military budget.'"

Home is in Fox Chapel, a suburb of Pittsburgh which, because it contains some large Irish American Catholic families, he once dubbed "No Pill Hill." His holiday and occasional business entertainment home is his County Kildare house, Castlemartin; and he has a retreat near Glandore in the wilds of West Cork. He and his wife enjoy Pittsburgh, "handsome, doughty, unusual and dramatic. An enormous amount of American industrial drama is taking place on the stage called Pittsburgh," he says.

Perhaps because of the seminal influence of Sir Basil Goulding who died recently, O'Reilly has an unusual interest in art. "Goulding, aesthete and athlete, patrician figure from the Victorian past, had an unorthodox quality of mind. He would have been a wonderful professor. He was able to achieve under pressure and he always displayed grace under pressure. We shared a love for the clerihew" (an esoteric form of Limerick) "and I admired his sense of the visual."

His special love is the school of Walter Osborne, the Irish artist who flourished in the late 19th century. He owns two very good Walter Osbornes which are hanging in Castlemartin. Osborne he regards as the greatest of the Irish Impressionists. O'Reilly is a patron of the Whitney Museum in New York, and the Heinz Foundation has given help to the National Gallery of Ireland. His friend and colleague Vincent Ferguson is a well-known collector and now owns the most important of Dublin's commercial art galleries, the Hendriks.

Let this Irishman of America have the last word himself: "Most Irish people share an awareness of the contradiction in the saying, 'the luck of the Irish.' The only great luck that ever befell them was emigration to the United States..."

JOSEPH A. ROCHE

UNDER the title of the St. Patrick's Fraternal Society, the Ancient Order of Hibernians established its first branch in the United States in 1836. Two years later, it was renamed the A.O.H. and has remained so to this day, when it is led by Joseph A. Roche and can claim 75,000 members, men, women and children.

The Irish A.O.H. worked well with the American A.O.H. until 1884, when there was a dispute over the admission of members of Irish descent instead of Irish birth. This dissension was copied by the Irish A.O.H., so that the Order was divided into two groups in each country and there were four executives. Both breaches were later healed, to be succeeded by other differences and today, although there are harmonious relations between the Orders in Ireland and America, there is as yet no formal constitutional link.

One is reminded of the story about the late Brenden Behan attending the inaugural meeting of the Kilmainham Jail Restoration Committee. "And now, Mr. Chairman", said Behan in his broad Dublin accent, "in the true Republican tradition, I'd like to propose—a split".

"To be admitted to membership, a man must be of Irish birth or Irish descent through either parent, a practising Catholic, and at least sixteen years of age". That is the wording of the current leaflet containing the membership application form, and this specific restriction causes President Roche to welcome warmly the establishment of an umbrella organisation such as the Irish American Unity Conference formed in 1983 by James A. Delaney and others. "I see the I.A.U.C. as a new initiative", says Roche, although it must be said that in May, 1984, he was reported in the *Irish World* as having abstained on an A.O.H. motion endorsing the I.A.U.C.

Roche's welcome at any rate does not mean that the A.O.H. has ceded its role as the leader of the Irish American community. "We are around the longest; we have the best record of accomplishment, and we have weathered a lot of storms", he says. "Our main task is to find a peaceful solution of the Northern Ireland problem through legitimate means. It was the A.O.H. which in 1979 asked Congressman Mario

Biaggi to form the Ad Hoc Congressional Committee for Irish Affairs, and that committee now has 104 members of both House and Senate.

"We knew we were winning when the Friends of Ireland committee was formed as a reaction to the Ad Hoc Committee. Now we have given honorary membership to Biaggi, who is a wonderful man, dedicated to peace and justice. I don't know why it's taken us so long to recognise him. He's certainly paid his dues".

The consistent stand of the Ancient Order of Hibernians in America on the Irish question is demonstrated by reference to a man who was no friend of Ireland or the A.O.H. In his book "The Secret Societies of Ireland: Their Rise and Progress" (Philip Allan, London, 1922), Captain H.B.C. Pollard, who is described as "late of the staff of the Chief of Police, Ireland", has this to say:

"The A.O.H. in America has for many years been under the direct control of the Clan-na-Gael, which also influences through the A.O.H. such American Catholic Associations as are not distinctly Irish, such as the *Knights of Columbus*, a Catholic Fraternal Society, in some ways akin to the Y.M.C.A. The A.O.H. of America is powerfully organised and has over six thousand lodges. . . . In 1908 the American A.O.H. was already in revolt against the Irish Parliamentary Party who controlled the A.O.H. in Ireland. At the 46th State Convention of the A.O.H. of Pennsylvania, the following declaration was made:-

"IRELAND

"That we again assert our unswerving fidelity to that fundamental principle of our Order, namely, the complete independence of Ireland, towards the attainment of which the untiring energy of all patriotic Irishmen should be directed; that is the meaning of the spirit of Irish nationality as all Hibernians understand it. We declare that Ireland is, under God, entitled to a free and independent form of Government, and the devoted struggle for liberty she has so long maintained has proven to the world her right of independence. We are convinced that nothing short of complete and absolute separation from England can ever bring lasting prosperity to Ireland".

Some 76 years later, the A.O.H. states: "We continue to support the efforts to create a unified Ireland, by the return of the six northeastern counties to the Republic Ireland". And Joe Roche says wistfully: "I wish we had some leaders who had some backbone. The present Taoiseach, Dr. FitzGerald, is fearful of any movement away from the centre. The best friend we have in Ireland is Charles Haughey who has exhibited a willingness to stand up to the British. I was in the Dáil in Dublin during the Malvinas/Falklands debate and I admired Haughey's stand on sanctions. 'You really showed courage', I told him afterwards.

"When I go to Ireland—and I've been there 14 or 15 times since our convention was held there in 1972—I usually send courtesy letters to the Taoiseach and the Foreign Minister asking them to see me and outlining what I'd like to talk about. Most recently, for example, I wanted to speak to them about Michael O'Rourke and a time frame for British withdrawal from the North. But since I attended the Noraid banquet in January, 1983, they write back and say that they are too busy to see me.

"They hurt themselves when they do this to me. I know they have problems. I know things like the economy get in the way. When Haughey was Taoiseach, I had a good relationship with him, though he warned me on the subject of Noraid. But he expressed his admiration for the work that Irish Americans were doing in bringing issues to the forefront, and for not being ambiguous".

On the question of Michael O'Rourke, the young man who was imprisoned in the United States for 55 months for the offence of "overstaying his visa, his only offence in the United States", as Roche tells it, he says:

"We needed a victory and one that we could have won within the law. We did not necessarily agree with what O'Rourke did."

[O'Rourke escaped to America from a Dublin courthouse in 1976 after his six-year conviction on charges of membership of the I.R.A. and possession of explosives, and was returned to the custody of the Irish authorities in June 1984. He was sentenced in October, 1984, to four years for escaping from the courthouse. He had pleaded guilty. President Roche was in court and said he was satisfied that O'Rourke was ready to turn over a new leaf.]

Speaking to the present writer in New York a month before the hearing, Roche said: "He was a fugitive from persecution and I would like to see recognition of the fact that he already has served five years. That would heal a lot of wounds.

"His wife, Margaret Lieb O'Rourke, whom he married in Philadelphia before he was arrested in 1979, has gone to Ireland to be near him, and his mother has told me in her home in Finglas, Dublin, that if he could get a two to three years' sentence, he would still be young enough when he was released to have a family. I believe Margie was being deprived of a basic human right—the love and comfort of her husband—while Michael was held in the United States".

The Noraid dinner was held six months before O'Rourke was returned to Ireland and on that occasion Roche said: "The previous Irish Government have said they are not out to get Michael, so which Government wants their pound of flesh? It can't be the United States, for we are the land of the free and the home of the brave. Use your imagination and you will see who the prime mover is in this travesty of justice. If we allow Michael to lose his fight for political asylum we will all lose some part of the freedom we have all gained because of our forefathers: if we allow a foreign power, England, to dictate to our Immigration Authorities through our State Department, we have permitted her to usurp a right that belongs to the American people".

It would be idle to deny that Joe Roche is a controversial figure on the landscape of Irish America. His address to the Irish Northern Aid dinner stated the A.O.H. position on the legitimate aspirations of the Irish people for independence; commended Noraid for "all the works of mercy that you perform for the prisoners and their families", and stated: "We, as a body, are opposed to violence and I personally abhor the use of force that causes so much misery and suffering to so many people. We, as an organisation, want to wipe out suffering on both sides of this conflict".

In an interview with *Magill* magazine in February, 1984, Joe Roche told Máire Crowe: "We in the A.O.H., we're opposed to all violence—R.U.C., I.R.A., U.D.A., but most importantly we're opposed to what the British army is up to. I think it would be fair to say that I.N.A., A.O.H. and the Unity Conference are now coming together more formally. Of course, you know that a lot of Noraid members are also members of the A.O.H."

The close observer of these words must be forgiven if he feels confused. Only three months before the Noraid dinner, James Delaney and his close associate in the Irish American Unity Conference, James P. Shannon, were among nine senior members of the Board of the A.O.H. who signed a strong statement condemning President Roche for transferring the annual A.O.H. convention from Galway "for frivolous and personal reasons", and "using appointed officers to overturn a democratic decision".

The convention, which was held eventually in Albany, New York, in July, saw a tussle for the Presidency between Roche and George J. Clough, who also had signed the October, 1983, statement. Clough lost. The *Connacht Tribune's* John Cunningham reckoned the loss of the convention to Galway at IR£1 million, the hotel bookings alone involving 900 bedrooms.

The fact is that Joseph A. Roche is President of the Ancient Order of Hibernians, elected at San Antonio, Texas, in 1982, and dedicated to decisive leadership, financial reform, improved communications and an increased membership.

At the 1978 Convention, held in Killarney, Roche was elected Chairman of the National Headquarters Committee, and three years later he had the satisfaction of seeing the A.O.H.'s first National Office opened on Wisconsin Avenue, Washington, D.C. Frank Duggan is the Legislative Counsel, the Capitol Hill lobbyist; Marianne Lacey is the Secretary; Pat O'Sullivan the Press Officer. In every month, Joe Roche spends three weekends away from his home in Baldwin, Maryland, and between the beginning of September and the end of January that frequency is increased to every weekend.

"My wife Lucille not only tolerates this deprivation of leisure time but is really interested in the development of the A.O.H. and often comes on visits with me. I could not do what I do without her. She came with me in February, 1984, when we experienced the greatest thrill I have had as a Hibernian and as National President. That was our visit to Belfast to honour the families of the hunger strikers. I think they were greatly encouraged by our presence. I made a visit to Long Kesh as well and I had an interview on Irish National Television which focused attention on our Order".

Aged 49, Joe Roche had three Irish grandparents. His father's people were from Cork City and his mother's from Ballymacarbery, Clonmel, County Tipperary. "The inspiration for my Irishness comes from my mother, who was a Republican", he says. "Her father left Ireland at 18 when he was accused of poaching the Queen's fish. He was a blacksmith and you can still see the ruins of his forge. It was she who made me join the A.O.H. because of the culture and the history behind it".

Roche's birthplace was Lawrenceville, Pittsburgh, a district known as "Irish Town". He went to St. Kieran's School and then to the Christian Brothers' (De La Salle) Central Catholic High School. He was awarded a degree in Business Administration at Johns Hopkins University, Baltimore, and also studied at Duquesne University, Pittsburgh.

He has been in life insurance for the whole 27 years of his working life. His company, Monumental Life, has its headquarters in Baltimore and he is now manager for the Baltimore area. Before that, he held a senior position as Field Vice President for Michigan and Ohio, but his commitment to the A.O.H. brought an end to that seven-year phase of his career and he opted for a position which would make it easier for him to fulfil his duties as National President.

"The Lord has been good to me", he reflects. "He has enabled me to make a very good living so that, while this post may be a financial sacrifice, it is not onerous in that way".

Joe Roche's wife is the former Lucille O'Neill, whose grandfather was from County Tyrone. When they married 30 years ago, Roche was still a student so his wife had to work. She was in the catering business and she still is, with the difference that now she owns the business, which covers weddings, bar mitzvahs and other social functions.

Their eldest daughter Colleen (29) was a department head in Roche's insurance firm. Now she is married to a professional photographer and works with her husband. Kim (27) is a registered nurse and works in the Mercy Hospital in Baltimore. Susan (25) is an assistant bank manager and is married to a farmer. Mary Patricia (23) is also married and has her own cleaning business. Louanne (22) is a computer programmer with her father's firm, and Joseph Michael (20) is a warehouseman. Four of their five daughters have been to Ireland, and at one time even thought of enrolling at University College, Cork.

Joe Roche has been a member of the Ancient Order of Hibernians for as long as he has been working. He has served with distinction at every level of the Order. As National Vice President he testified in the U.S. Senate in favour of a Bill to preserve a unique forest in south-east Missouri known as the Irish Wilderness, a huge wooded area rich in wildlife and unusual beauty and consisting of 17,000 acres.

The area got its name when an immigrant priest, Father John Hogan, sought to build a permanent settlement for the poor Irish labourers in the railroad camps of St. Louis in 1858. The dream crumbled with the onset of the Civil War, leaving only the name, the Irish Wilderness, to history.

Another of Roche's achievements as Vice President was the recognition by Congress of Commodore John Barry as the real father of the American Navy. President Reagan signed the Bill into law in 1981 through the efforts of Roche and his committee including Frank Duggan, the A.O.H.'s legislative counsel. Commodore John Barry Day has, says Roche, joined St. Patrick's Day and Independence Day as one of the Order's "holy days". It is celebrated on September 13th, the anniversary of Barry's death.

A project near to Joe Roche's heart is the erection of an obelisk in the Medal of Honor Grove at Valley Forge, Pennsylvania, to commemorate the 66 Irishmen who won the Congressional Medal of Honor in the Civil War and the Indian Campaigns. "These men, like some British and Norwegians who are in the same category, are stateless. That is to say, their names cannot be inscribed on the obelisks of any State of the Union because when they died they did not belong to any State. This project was initiated by the Curator of the Medal of Honor Grove, Sister Marie Veronica, who is the archivist and found their names. We are pretty close to ground-breaking on the project and we have nearly raised the $10,000 necessary.

"One of the reasons that I am proud to be involved in this commemoration at the Freedoms Foundation at Valley Forge is that it counters the feeling that all we in the A.O.H. are concerned about is the Republican Movement", says President Roche and he quotes a newspaper editorial: "The persons who have heard forests praying and who know that only God can make a tree, will find their inspiration in the grove itself. There they can match the exhilarating inspiration of His botanical work with the singular greatness He has bestowed upon those men who possess the qualities to earn a Medal of Honor".

The influence of the A.O.H. is felt in every community where a division of the Order exists—and there are at least 75 more divisions since Roche became National Organiser in 1978. The financial roll of honour over the years has been impressive. The order has distributed over $27 million in sick benefits; $13 million in death benefits, and about $10 million for charitable purposes.

In 1906 the victims of the San Francisco earthquake were given $44,000. The Boer Ambulance Corps benefited by $10,000 and in education $50,000 went to the establishment of a chair of Celtic Languages at the Catholic University of Washington; $44,000 to the Catholic Church Extension Society, and $44,000 to the Irish College in Rome. Countless other appeals were heard and continue to be heard in the spirit of the Order's motto; "Friendship, Unity and Christian Charity".

No Hibernian President before Joe Roche has travelled so widely on behalf of the Order. He has made well over 100 out-of-state visits since his election, journeying not only to Ireland but to Alaska and Canada "to spread the word" and working steadily to achieve his aim of doubling the membership of the Ancient Order of Hibernians by 1990. The Order is in good heart to celebrate its sesquicentennial in 1986.

KEVIN ROCHE

IN 1922, just as a short and bitter civil war was beginning in Ireland, Éamonn Kevin Roche was born in Dublin. In the same year, at the age of 49, Eliel Saarinen from Finland launched his American career with a second prize in the international competition for a skyscraper for the *Chicago Tribune*. Now Kevin Roche is one of the world's leading architects and the heir to the American architectural practice that Saarinen's son Eero left when he died suddenly in 1961.

Kevin Roche's father, who had voted against the Treaty with England in January, 1922, was in Limerick Jail when his son was born. It was his second imprisonment—the first was in an English jail before the Truce—and he was a member of the Dáil, the Irish Parliament, at the time. He was jailed because he was an organiser for the Irish Republican Army. He was from Bansha in County Tipperary, and his wife, Alice Harding Roche, was a native of Tipperary town.

After the Civil War, Éamon Roche (like Éamon de Valera, who grew up in Bruree, County Limerick, next door to Roche, he spelled his name with one "n") became manager of a small co-operative creamery in Mitchelstown, County Cork. By the time he died in 1953, he had used his phenomenal organising ability to develop Mitchelstown into a multi-million pound business processing milk into cheese, lactose, chocolate crumb and milk powder and making an international reputation. He and his wife had two other sons, Paud, who died in 1983 and was a solicitor in Mitchelstown, and Pierce, who after a lifetime in the motor trade has retired to run a summer sailing rescue programme on the River Shannon.

After school in Mitchelstown, Kevin Roche went to Rockwell College in Cashel, where in 1938 he discovered and laboured through John Ruskin's *The Seven Lamps of Architecture*. "When we build, let us think that we build forever", Ruskin wrote, and Roche was fascinated and impressed.

A year later, when he was 17, he got the opportunity to design a building, a small warehouse, and he was able to work on it during construction. "It was enough to get me very deeply involved in architecture", he says. The following year, as Mitchelstown Creameries grew, he designed a series of substantial farm buildings for a new method of raising animals on a liquid diet. As the complex ultimately housed 8,000 animals it needed elaborate systems of feed and waste-matter distribution.

In 1940 when Roche became a student, the school of architecture in University College, Dublin, was headed by Professor Rudolf Maximilian Butler, a German-trained architect who was an advocate of the Beaux Arts school. Roche in 1982 told Philip Jodidio of *Connaissance des Arts*: "At a time when they were teaching most American architectural students to scorn the lessons of the past, I had to draw acanthus leaves and classical columns. In Dublin, we got a very rigorous and classical training".

Butler died in 1941 and for many of Roche's student days, the college carried on without a professor of architecture. They were happy years for him, those war years in neutral Ireland. He lived over the Monument Creameries in Upper Baggot Street. The shop was one of a chain owned by his aunt, Mrs. Ryan, and among his neighbours he numbered Patrick Kavanagh the poet, who had not yet begun to write; Brian O'Nolan, whose famous column An Cruiskeen Lawn had just begun to appear in *The Irish Times* under the pseudonym Myles na gCopaleen, and Patrick Campbell, later Lord Glenavy, the journalist and writer.

Among his fellow students were Patrick Scott, now a well-known artist; Dan O'Herlihy the film actor and director whose son worked with Roche for some time recently; and Kevin Fox and Wilfrid Cantrell, the Dublin architects. His literary mentor was James Joyce and he can still recite long chapters of *Finnegans Wake*, the work given, as Harry Levin has said, "to a world bewildered by other enigmas in 1939".

Graduating from the National University of Ireland in 1945, he went to work for Michael Scott, the leading architect in Ireland. There was a construction boom after the war and Roche worked on some large projects that were in design—the bus station, the Donnybrook bus garage, ("very advanced for its day"); some office buildings.

In 1946 he went to London briefly to work with Maxwell Fry on education buildings in Africa. Fry had worked with Walter Gropius and he and F.R.S. Yorke, Tecton, Mendelsoln and Chermayeff were the leading English designers of the post-war period. "Working with Max Fry was a wonderful experience and made me feel that I should go to graduate school". He applied to Harvard, where Gropius was; to Yale and to the Illinois Institute of Technology where Ludwig Mies van der

Rohe was teaching. "I decided on Mies finally because of the impression his work had made on me. There was a kind of morality and discipline in his work which I had never experienced in design before. But I ran out of funds and after a tour of the West Coast where I visited all of Frank Lloyd Wright's buildings and Neutra's and the Greene brothers' and Maybeck's buildings in San Francisco, I took a job as a office boy in the United Nations planning office. After a vacation at home I returned to find that I had been laid off".

If you ask Kevin Roche what brought him to America in the first place, he answers: "I don't know how honest to be about that question. First, I suppose, an industrial country is where an architect has to be; secondly, it was very difficult to be successful in Ireland where the environment did not encourage success. It's a very tough thing to overcome, though of course that may have all changed in the meantime. Thirdly, I had a sense of frustration in Ireland, and fourthly there was the isolation of the war years at a critical age in my life. I felt locked in and I wanted to learn something about modern architecture, which did not exist in Professor Butler's mind. I had to relearn, and it was good. I was 26 when I emigrated from Shannon Airport to Chicago".

After a few months' unemployment, Kevin Roche was hired by Eero Saarinen, by sheer coincidence joining the firm in the same week as John Dinkeloo, who was to become Roche's partner after Saarinen's death. Although Dinkeloo himself died in 1981 at the age of 63, his extraordinary talents live on in the name of the firm, Kevin Roche John Dinkeloo and Associates.

"John" says Roche, "was a truly remarkable architect. He had great skills, a great sense of construction. He was very pragmatic and had a good business sense, but he had great courage and great vision...He was Eero's partner from 1950 to 1961 and ran the entire production for almost all of the jobs.

"In the process John developed many products such as reflecting glass and weathering steel, which rusts to a certain point and then seals itself. John's great attribute was that he really had no ambition to design, but he was completely supportive...It wasn't that he did not have feelings about the character of a building—he set for himself where he was going to perform".

During the 1950s Eero Saarinen and Associates became perhaps the pre-eminent corporate architectural firm in the United States. Saarinen exploited the new structural technologies and sought to provide a unique architectural form to meet the requirements of each client. The synthesis produced some of the most visually arresting buildings constructed in the 20th century.

When Saarinen died in 1961, Kevin Roche, since 1955 his chief design associate, and John Dinkeloo, in charge of the firm's technical development, completed their mentor's ten unfinished designs, among them the granite-clad CBS tower in Manhattan; Dulles International Airport outside Washington, D.C., the TWA terminal at Kennedy Airport, and what is regarded as Saarinen's finest late work, the Deere and Company headquarters in Moline, Illinois.

The firm moved from an outer suburb of Detroit to Hamden, Connecticut, which had been Saarinen's intention, and in 1966 complied with his wish to have his name removed from the firm. In Hamden, Roche works with a staff of 90—"the same number more or less for 30 years"—in a Victorian mansion, overlooking a reservoir and built by a German cigar maker who, it is said, wanted a kind of castle on the Rhine.

But Roche was still in Detroit when in 1961 the partners won their first independent commission against 37 international architects. The city of Oakland in California wanted to build three museums: art, natural history and history. Roche decided to house all three in one structure with floors and roofs arranged to form a public park. Thus down-at-heel down-town Oakland was transformed and its people given a common meeting place. Most of the four-block complex is tucked under roof gardens and terraces linked by stairways, walks and intersecting plazas.

The garden created outside in Oakland was put inside the Ford Foundation building in Manhattan, where the greenery lies in a courtyard of glass taller than the nave of Amiens Cathedral. "We thought it very important", Roche says, "for people to be aware of each other visually. This is often neglected in work environments, though not of course in homes".

That commission launched Roche and Dinkeloo as innovators in office-building designs, many of which are still under construction. The latest to be noticed critically outside the professional magazines was the Union Carbide building in Danbury Connecticut, which was remarked on by *Newsweek* in May, 1984. "Architects of the stature of Kevin Roche and Araldo Cossutta are among the leaders of a new post-industrial design", said the magazine in a five-page feature on "Offices of the Future".

At Union Carbide, Roche began by interviewing employees at all levels and came up with the fact that the company was ensnared in a system that demanded nine different office sizes and a range of furnishings and accoutrements. "Here were these mature, honourable people", he says, "being subjected to and administering a kind of kindergarten system at costs that were sapping their finances and energies".

He persuaded management to scrap this pyramid of perquisites and give all staff members the same size office, about 13 feet square. But he so designed the building that everyone has a room with a view over the Danbury countryside. The offices are conceived of as private dens. An elaborate computer programme was developed that allowed each employee to choose his own appointments—desks, lamps, carpets, pictures, everything—from a range of 30 interchangeable sets. Apart from the design savings Roche effected, the company has done away with the $1.2 million a year that used to be entailed in moving partitions to accommodate status changes.

"People enjoy the building, they like using it, and they relate to it. It was designed as buildings ought to be designed. The process was absolutely flawless".

Union Carbide is different from, say, Roche's General Foods headquarters at Rye, New York, which demanded to be seen. "In the 19th century, when someone bought a pot of marmalade they might see an image of the factory where it was made printed on the outside of the jar.... There was a desire to establish reliablility, permanence, reputation through the qualities of the building. Now it will be very hard to think of General Foods without thinking of its headquarters", says Roche.

The best known building in the United States is the White House in Washington, D.C., which was designed by another Irishman, James Hoban, and it is not perhaps coincidental that General Foods with its central pavilion, columns and symmetrical colonnaded wings shares the Palladian manner with Hoban's building.

Roche outlines his philosophy: "As a design develops, I ask myself constantly: 'Are we really designing for the people who will use this building?' That is part of the process of maturing, because as a young architect, at least in the period that I grew up in, I never heard anybody mention people. It was as if people were a nuisance in buildings, and it would be nice if one could build and not have to take them into consideration. The feeling seemed to be prevalant that not only were they a nuisance when one was trying to evolve a design, but when the building was built, they just messed it up. So, in the purist approach of the late 40s and the 50s, people were not always the final priority of the architect".

Roche's partners, Philip Kinsella and James Owens, have shared with him the honours that have been heaped on them, prizes, awards, medals, both domestic and international. In 1982 came the accolade, the Pritzger Architecture Prize, for which the jury included J. Carter Brown, Director of the National Gallery of Art in Washington; Philip Johnson, winner of the 1979 Pritzger Prize, and five other members of similar standing.

In his acceptance address, Roche gave thanks "to this great free community, the United States and those other free communities which make it possible for us all to live and work in freedom in a world where the concept of individual freedom is given much lip service but where it exists as a reality only in a few fortunate places..... We should, all of us, bend our will to create a civilisation in which we can live at peace with nature and each other. To build well is an act of peace. Let us hope that it will not be in vain".

Of the more than 50 corporate and public projects designed and built well by Kevin Roche since 1961, it has been possible to mention only a few in this space. His simple and elegant architecture does not lend itself to classification by those who, as Philip Jodidio has said, "would separate contemporary architects into opposing camps and hang silly labels on them from 'pre'- to 'post'- and points between. The truth is rarely so simple. We can sum up Roche's technique in the same terms as he has used to describe the General Foods project. 'It is neither modern nor post-modern. It makes itself felt by its presence'".

Talking to Jodidio in 1982, Roche said: "*L'engagement social des premiers architectes modernes a été perdu depuis longtemps, et je pense que c'est regrettable. Il faudra que nous retrouvions cette voie*". It is at least arguable that Roche already has renewed the social commitment of the early modern architects.

On June 10th, 1963, Kevin Roche at 41 married Jane Tuohy of Ohio. She had been a designer in Saarinen's office. Perhaps that is why their friends tend to be architects. They live near the office in Hamden, in a pleasant house which was the stable belonging to Eli Whitney the inventor. They have five children, a dog and a cat, and they keep a little summer house about 20 minutes away on Long Island. The family move out there in the summer and Roche commutes. "I don't take vacations", he says. But he loves to cook.

Their eldest son, Éamon (with one 'n' like his grandfather) is 20 and at Columbia University. He enjoys rowing, English literature and sculpture. Paud (18) is at High School in Hamden and is very interested in literature and acting. Denis, aged 17, christened herself years ago. Once upon a time she was Mary. Now she is at the American School in Lugano, Switzerland, but she will finish high school in America. Anne, who is 15, is in tenth grade and Alice (13) is in junior high, both at a local private school.

Paud, who is called after his uncle, spent the whole summer of 1983 cycling around Ireland, staying at bed and breakfast houses and in architect Robin Walker's house in County Kerry. "The children all like to go to Ireland every couple of years", Roche says. "They are very conscious of that aspect of their heritage. I don't want to make them schizophrenic about Ireland but they have a deep interest nevertheless.

"I've always avoided the intensely Irish community here because it seems foolish to come to another country and try to remain Irish. If you emigrated in the 1940s you were not accepted by Irish Americans". He became a naturalised American citizen in 1964.

Tall, balding, humorous and looking very much younger than 62, Kevin Roche the architect and the man have been encapsulated by the anonymous writer of the Pritzger Prize citation:

"In this mercurial age, when our fashions swing overnight from the severe to the ornate, from contempt for the past to nostalgia for imagined times that never were, Kevin Roche's formidable body of work sometimes intersects fashion, sometimes lags fashion, and more often makes fashion.

"He is no easy man to describe: an innovator who does not worship innovation for itself; a professional unconcerned with trends, a quiet humble man who conceives and executes great works, a generous man of strictest standards for his own work.

"In this award to Kevin Roche we recognise and honour an architect who persists in being an individual, and has for all of us, through his work and his person, made a difference for the better".

EUGENE J. SULLIVAN

WHEN Eugene J. Sullivan left the United States Navy at the end of World War II, he went looking for a job alphabetically. "I went to American Airlines, Borden and Coca-Cola", he says. "Borden's offered me a job and I tore up the rest of my list. I could have ended up at Xerox".

Gene Sullivan has been at Borden's ever since and by 1979 had become Chairman and Chief Executive Officer. When he was asked at the time for his reaction to his election he said: "I've been married to the same girl for 36 years; I worked for the same company for 34 years, and I've lived in New York City for 58 years. You might say that stick-to-it-iveness pays off". More quietly now, and conscious of the fact that over 35% of Corporate America is controlled by Irish Americans, he will tell you that he is the first Irish Chairman ever.

Borden, Inc., is an international food, dairy and chemical corporation with sales last year of $4.26 billion and a worldwide workforce of 32,000. In Ireland, it has plants at Mallow, County Cork, making milk powder, and in Athy, County Kildare, making metal cans.

Gene Sullivan's first action, initiated within a month of his assuming command, was a major restructuring of the company. "We decided we would eliminate our low-return commodity businesses", he says, "and we sold off roughly 20% of the firm's operations in a move to finance a $1.5 billion investment in our strongest businesses".

Sullivan's move was seen by Wall Street analysts as "a bold step committing the company to growth in the areas it understands", and Borden is now repositioned as a strong consumer products company and an efficient supplier of chemicals for specialty uses.

One of the leaders in the development of new food products to meet present-day health concerns with low-fat, low-calorie and low-sodium brands in traditional areas such as cheeses and other dairy-based products, snacks and soups, Borden has seen its earnings per share rise steadily through the past three years. As a mark of recognition of Gene Sullivan's development programme, the market doubled the value of Borden stock well in advance of the 1983 bull market.

It would be impossible to describe the variety of food and chemical products that Borden markets. Even in Europe, for example, Suzy, the Belgian bakery operation, is a Borden company that is the world's largest producer of waffles with 50% of the Belgian market and exports throughout the continent. Cocio is the leading brand of bottled chocolate milk in Denmark, and the Weber bakery in Germany is the supplier of hamburger buns to McDonald's chain of restaurants in that country. In Asia, Lady Borden continues to dominate the premium ice-cream market in Japan.

Like all American companies of comparable size, Borden has a conduit for charitable contributions. The Borden Foundation Inc. has a special interest in higher education and supports Independent College Funds of America and the United Negro College Fund, which together represent 622 institutions of higher learning. The company, to which Sullivan early on appointed a Director of Corporate Social Responsibility, also says that over the last six years the participation of minorities and women in its workforce has risen by more than 35%, and that a further improvement in representation is envisaged. Two of its 13 directors are women. Virginia Dwyer is senior vice president, finance, of the American Telephone and Telegraph Company (AT and T), and Patricia Carry Stewart is vice president of the Edna McConnell Clark Foundation, a charitable foundation.

The Consumer Products Division of Borden at present operates 101 manufacturing and processing facilities in the United States and Puerto Rico; and the International Division has 20 food and dairy manufacturing and processing facilities, principally in Latin America and Western Europe. The Chemical Division operates 48 facilities in the United States and the Consumer Products Division has three consumer chemical plants in the U.S. and Canada. The International Division operates 39 chemical manufacturing and processing plants located principally in Brazil and Western Europe. That seems to add up to 211 facilities worldwide, with a new concentration on the dairy business in the Sun Belt of the South and Southwest where, as Gene Sullivan says, "it's been benefiting from population growth, a more favourable winter climate and, frankly, stronger Borden brand loyalty".

Sullivan is an early riser who does his best work at 7 a.m. "I believe that late night sessions don't produce a person's best", he says. "When we were devising our new strategy, we had a lot of watch-the-sun-come-up meetings". Some of these meetings were in his office where on the wall behind his desk he has a picture of Gail Borden, the founder. The company's administrative headquarters are in Columbus, Ohio, but its executive offices are on Park Avenue, New York. "You might say I'm a Big Apple person", he says.

His fellow Irish American and classmate from St. John's University, Hugh Carey, asked him in 1980 to chair the Governor's Council for International Business.

"The idea", he says, "was to try to encourage the growth of international business in New York and to try to encourage exports from New York". For this two years of work Governor Carey offered no salary; nor has there been any money in Gene Sullivan's other voluntary work—for example, as chairman of the board of St. Francis Hospital in Roslyn, New York, where his wife Gloria has also been active. He quotes Oscar Wilde: "A cynic is someone who knows the price of everything and the value of nothing", and he adds: "Being a volunteer has great value, and you can't put a price on it".

His greatest unpaid endeavour is sharing his rich business experience with young people coming up. In 1973, he established the first Executive-in-Residence programme at St. John's University's School of Business Administration. Each semester some 20 to 30 advanced students meet with Sullivan and many of his key executives to analyse actual business situations. Once each semester they finish their study in the Borden boardroom, deliberating over an investment proposal that has been presented to the company and making their own decisions on whether or not to approve it.

Gene Sullivan has also served as co-chairman of a key panel in the President's Private Sector Survey on Cost Control, a group charged by President Reagan with finding ways to make the federal government more cost-effective. Sullivan's panel found ways of recouping some $36 billion of tax-payers' money through user charges for certain key federal functions. It is characteristic of the man that his panel came down as heavily on business freeloaders at the federal service trough as on any other group.

Eugene Sullivan was born in Brooklyn and grew up in Queens. His mother was from the County Cavan side of the road from Granard to Ballyjamesduff. She carried the Cavan name of Smith, though she had a cousin who spelt it Smyth. Her people were tenant farmers.

His father left Lauratuosist on the Kenmare River in County

Kerry, when he was 18. His own father had worked for the local landowner. Gene Sullivan's father died at 87; his mother is 96. The last uncle in Ireland died four years ago, but there are cousins there and in England. He has only one brother, John.

Mrs. Sullivan was strongly influenced in the Astoria section of Queen's by a neighbouring family called Connolly. Joe Connolly is a lawyer and impressed upon her the necessity for making sure that Gene Sullivan went to college. At St. John's University in Queens he took a degree in business studies. That was in 1942, and he went straight into the Navy, where he had become a full lieutenant when he was discharged in December, 1945.

That is when the alphabetical career choice was made and he joined Borden as a sales trainee with the Chemical Division. Sales suited him because as a student he had enjoyed part-time salesmanship at Macy's and Abraham & Straus.

He worked at night for an MBA from New York University and in 1950 got his degree with a major in marketing. His *alma mater*, St. John's, awarded him an honorary Ph.D. in 1973, the year he became an adjunct professor at the School of Business and founded the Executive-in-Residence programme. His advice to aspiring graduates is: "Always do more than is expected of you to rise above the group you are peered with".

Gene Sullivan's rise in the Borden Company was rapid, and by December, 1967, he had become a director and a member of the executive committee. He was elected President in 1973, and he retained that title when he became Chairman and Chief Executive Officer. He has a number of outside directorships including Warner Lambert, the F.W. Woolworth Co., and the Bank of New York, which celebrates its bicentenary in 1984. He is also a member of the Council on Foreign Relations.

He is married to the former Gloria Roesch, "a girl I've known since I was 14 in Astoria. She's Irish-German (her mother was a Quinn) and that's the best combination you can get". They have four children and several grandchildren. Nobody in the family speaks Irish but Sullivan's father taught his son to bless himself in Irish. His good friend Cardinal Tomás Ó Fiaich of Armagh has heard his prayer and pronounced it fine—"but you have left the Son out of the Trinity".

A friend and colleague says of Gene Sullivan: "He's just made a huge difference in the company. His predecessor and he have brought us into the 20th century. Before that we were all old-fashioned milk people. To go peddle a fifth of your company is not an easy thing to do. The jobs stayed all right, but under different owners.

"Gene Sullivan has turned the place around. He doesn't do much horn-tooting, but he takes what he gets into very actively and very seriously. He's a member of the American Irish Historical Society and he was one of the two questioners at the Economic Club dinner which was addressed by Charles Haughey as Taoiseach. The other questioner was Senator Daniel Patrick Moynihan".

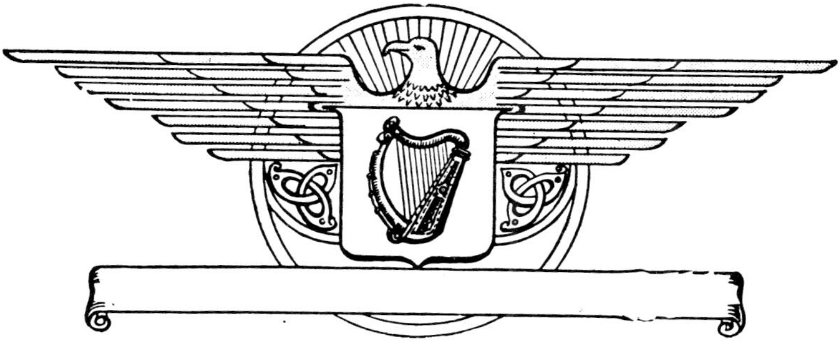

A piece of serendipity. I found this printing block in a New York street market while I was researching *Dreamers of Dreams*. The stallholder knew nothing of its history, but to me it seemed an appropriate symbol of the Irish in America.

D.O'D.

INDEX